Small Talk BIG Impact

Learn How to Be Charismatic and Talk to Anyone, Overcome Anxiety, Improve Conversation Skills and Boost Confidence to Connect with People (Communication Skills Book)

Ava Priestley

Copyright © 2023 by Ava Priestley

All rights reserved. No part of this publication may be reproduced, stored in a retrieval system, or transmitted in any form or by any means, electronic, mechanical, photocopying, recording, scanning, or otherwise, without the prior written permission of the author.

Limit of Liability/Disclaimer of Warranty: This publication is designed to provide accurate and authoritative information in regard to the subject matter covered. It is sold with the understanding that neither the author nor the publisher is engaged in rendering legal, investment, accounting or other professional services. While the publisher and author have used their best efforts in preparing this book, they make no representations or warranties with respect to the accuracy or completeness of the contents of this book and specifically disclaim any implied warranties of merchantability or fitness for a particular purpose. No warranty may be created or extended by sales representatives or written sales materials. The advice and strategies contained herein may not be suitable for your situation. You should consult with a professional when appropriate.

The resources in this book are provided for informational purposes only and should not be used to replace the specialized training and professional judgment of a health care or mental health care professional.

Neither the publisher nor the author shall be liable for any loss of profit or any other commercial damages, including but not limited to special, incidental, consequential, personal, or other damages.

Small Talk Big Impact

Learn How to Be Charismatic and Talk to Anyone, Overcome Anxiety, Improve Conversation Skills and Boost Confidence to Connect with People

By Ava Priestley

[ISBN] *only needed for print books*

ACKNOWLEDGMENTS

First and foremost, my heartfelt gratitude goes to my mother, Sheila. Your wisdom, encouragement, and unwavering faith in me have been the guiding light and an endless source of inspiration, and for that, I am forever thankful.

To my partner, Jonny, thank you for standing by me with such patience and understanding. Your support has been a pillar of strength, and your belief in my work has fuelled my resolve. You have been a partner in every sense, sharing in both the challenges and triumphs.

To my siblings, words fall short to express my appreciation for your unconditional love and support. Your encouragement, humour, and comfort have been pillars in this journey. I am deeply grateful for your enduring presence and support.

This book is not just a reflection of my efforts but a testament to the love and support that each of you has generously provided. Thank you for being my family, my cheerleaders, and my foundation.

TABLE OF CONTENTS

INTRODUCTION 1

PART 1 5

    Small Talk with A Big Impact 6

    Chit-Chat Around the World: How Different Cultures Do Small Talk 10

    Digital Small Talk: Mastering Communication in the Age of Social Media and Texting 27

    Finding Your Voice: For the Shy, Introverted & Socially Awkward 38

    The Brain's Role in Human Connection and Social Interaction 46

PART 2 52

    The Good, The Bad & The Gabby: Unpacking What Makes a Good (Or Not So Good) Communicator 53

    Charisma and Confidence: The Winning Duo in Small Talk 58

    Beyond Words: Exploring Body Language, Facial Expressions and Tonality in Conversation 65

    Breaking the Ice: Crafting Perfect Conversation Starters 73

    Navigating Group Conversations: Strategies for Engaging Multiple People 83

    Navigating Complexities: Dealing with Difficult People 92

    Oops, That Was Awkward: How to Bounce Back from Conversation Fumbles 99

The Art of the Exit 105

PART 3 112

Saying Sorry in Small Talk and Beyond 113

Judge Not: The Essential Virtue of Non-Judgment in Conversation 123

The Most Interesting Person in the Room: How to Become Fascinating to Others 131

Conclusion The Journey of Connection 135

THANKS FOR READING! 137

INTRODUCTION

Small talk is often regarded as a basic, even trivial aspect of our daily conversations. So routine, we don't even realise we engage in it. For many, small talk is often seen as the filler of our interactions, a superficial exchange of pleasantries before getting to the "real" conversation. It's those fleeting comments we make passing a neighbour in the driveway, waiting in line at a fast-food restaurant or talking to a colleague during a lunch break, that so many dismiss as mere idle chatter.

In a world that values depth and meaningful connections, many underestimate the power of small talk. This underestimation overlooks the foundational role that small talk plays in human communication. It acts as the initial spark that can ignite and lead to lasting connections and relationships. It serves as the bridge that brings people together from diverse backgrounds and walks of life. It's the gateway to opportunities and advancements and plays a pivotal role in the intricate tapestry of our social interactions. Underestimating its value would be missing the subtle yet profound ways it shapes our relationships and daily encounters.

Whether it's a casual comment about the weather, a friendly inquiry about someone's weekend, or a shared laugh over a cup of coffee, small talk has the power to enrich lives and turn ordinary moments into opportunities for connection and understanding.

But what exactly makes small talk an art?

While traditional educational systems often cover various communication skills, the nuances of casual conversation isn't always given the emphasis and attention it truly deserves. This gap can leave many individuals unaware and less equipped for the spontaneous or informal moments of our lives. This is why, in the pages that follow, we'll explore the nuances of small talk, offering insights, techniques, and practical advice to help you master this essential aspect of communication. Whether you're a seasoned conversationalist or someone looking to improve your social skills, this journey into the art of small talk promises to be enlightening and empowering.

Who Can Benefit from This Book?

At first glance, one might assume that a book on small talk is tailored primarily for those who struggle with social interactions. However, the truth is, the insights and strategies presented here have a broad appeal and can be invaluable to a wide range of readers.

The Networking Professional: Regular attendees of business events, conferences, and seminars understand the significance of first impressions. Mastering small talk is crucial, as it serves as a catalyst in establishing rapport, creating meaningful professional relationships, and uncovering opportunities that can influence their career trajectory.

The Social Butterfly: Even the most socially adept can enhance their conversational prowess. If you're someone who naturally thrives in social environments, there's always room to further hone your conversational skills, ensuring you leave lasting, positive impressions on those you interact with.

The Job Seeker: Job interviews often start with small talk. These initial exchanges, while seemingly casual, play an important role in setting the tone. By honing this skill, applicants can create a favourable first impression, laying a positive foundation for the more in-depth discussions that follow.

The Introvert: If social interactions aren't your strong suit, this book provides strategies and techniques to guide you through conversations with ease, all whilst boosting your confidence in social scenarios.

The Globetrotter: For those who love to travel, understanding the nuances of small talk can help in forging connections with locals and bridging the cultural gap, enhancing the travel experience.

The Lifelong Learner: If you're someone who believes in continuous personal development, refining your conversational skills is a valuable addition to your repertoire. By sharpening these skills, you not only enrich personal interactions but also add a vital tool to your ever-evolving personal growth toolkit.

Essentially, anyone who interacts with others—whether personally or professionally—stands to gain from the insights shared in this book. After all, every conversation, no matter how brief, has the potential to impact our lives in unexpected and meaningful ways.

How to Use This Book

Mastering the art of conversation might seem like a tall order, but this book is here to provide comfort and guide you every step of the way. My primary goal is to provide genuine and practical advice to help you deepen relationships and achieve your personal objective. This isn't about manipulation or trickery; it's about fostering real connections. Here's how you can make the most of this resource:

1. Start at Your Own Pace: While the chapters follow a logical progression, you're encouraged to explore sections that align with your immediate interests or challenges, as every reader's journey

is unique.

2. Engage Actively with Exercises: Scattered throughout the book are practical exercises and strategies. Dive into them. They're designed to help you transition from theory to actionable skills.

3. Take Moments to Reflect: This book is full of information. After reading each chapter, take a moment to pause and reflect on the insights you've gathered. Consider keeping a journal to capture your thoughts, personal anecdotes, or topics you'd like to explore further.

4. Apply in Real-Life Scenarios: The essence of mastering communication lies in real-world application. Challenge yourself to use your newfound knowledge in your daily interactions.

5. Revisit as Needed: Like any other, communication benefits from repetition and review. Don't hesitate to revisit chapters or sections that resonate with you or pose challenges.

6. Engage in Conversations About Conversations: Share your learnings and experiences with friends, family members or colleagues. Discussing these concepts can offer fresh perspectives and further solidify your understanding.

7. Maintain an Open Mind: The realm of interpersonal commu-nication is vast. As you navigate this book, remain open to the idea that there's always something new to uncover.

Above all, remember that the heart of this book is to empower you to build genuine relationships and enrich your interactions. With commitment and practice, you'll not only refine your conversational abilities but also unlock the countless joys and opportunities that come with heartfelt communication.

PART 1

Small Talk with A Big Impact

Small talk is essentially the skill of engaging in brief, casual conversations on topics that are typically considered light and non-controversial. While these conversations may appear simple on the surface, they serve a deeper purpose beyond just filling silence. They're about recognising our shared human experience. It's the process of finding common ground and building a bridge, however temporary, between two or more individuals. It's a way to acknowledge others, to say, "I see you, and I'm interested in engaging with you, even if just for a moment."

Far from being superficial, small talk is a subtle dance that requires attentiveness, empathy, and genuine interest in others. It's the grease that keeps the wheels of social interaction turning smoothly and the thread that weaves the fabric of our daily interactions, enabling us to move through various social settings with grace and ease. At its heart, small talk is a celebration of the ordinary, a way to find joy and connection in the mundane. It's a skill that can enhance our lives, foster community, and remind us that we are part of a larger whole. While it may not lead to profound revelations or deep connections every time, it's an essential aspect of human interaction that brings warmth and humanity to our everyday lives.

The fundamental aim of small talk is to forge bonds and establish a connection, especially in new or unfamiliar settings. It allows individuals to gauge each other's personalities, feelings, and intentions. Such as being at a social gathering, like a friend's party where you only recognise the host. Here, small talk becomes your compass, guiding you as you navigate the room, introduce yourself, and interact with others. A casual remark on the music or the decor can be the key that unlocks conversations, leading to the discovery of common interests, shared laughter, and a feeling of connectedness. Or similarly, walking into a room full of strangers at a business conference. The room buzzes with chatter, yet you're on the sidelines. Initiating small talk with a comment about the venue or a compliment about a presentation can break the ice and create an entry point, easing the atmosphere and making the environment more relaxed and approachable. In the world of romance and dating, small talk plays a crucial role, particularly during initial meetings such as a first date. These initial interactions, assist in setting both individuals at ease. They provide an opportunity to assess compatibility, discern potential chemistry and set the stage for more intimate, personal conversations. In all these examples, small talk lays the foundation for the relationship, however brief it might be. It set the groundwork for more profound and significant exchanges.

If you're still asking '*why exactly is mastering small talk so crucial?*' My response to you is, well beyond the immediate benefits of easing social tension and building connections, it's a skill that can open doors, both literally and metaphorically.

In the professional world, small talk often paves the way to new prospects and opportunities. Picture yourself at a networking event, surrounded by potential clients, hiring managers, or future partners. Skilfully initiating and sustaining casual conversations can potentially evolve into significant ties, uncover job opportunities or partner collaborations that might not have emerged otherwise. It's not merely the content of your words, but the manner in which you convey them. Demonstrating curiosity, posing intriguing questions, and practising attentive listening can leave a lasting impression, setting you apart in a competitive environment. In personal encounters, small talk is often the seed from which friendships grow. It's the shared laughter over a funny observation at an event, or the mutual interest discovered during a relaxed conversation at a local café, that can lead to a lifelong relationship. These seemingly minor interactions can light up our social life, creating a sense of community and belonging. Even going about our daily life, small talk has the power to transform our day. An unexpected compliment or a friendly exchange can automatically lift our spirits and change our mood, adding a touch of warmth and positivity to ordinary moments.

Furthermore, mastering small talk demonstrates social awareness, empathy, and adaptability. It shows that you're attuned to social cues, that you can adjust your communication style to different audiences, and that you're willing to step out of your comfort zone to engage with others. These qualities are valued in both personal and professional environments as it showcases emotional intelligence and a willingness to connect.

The good news is that small talk is a teachable skill. While some might naturally be more adept at it, anyone can learn and improve with practice and guidance. It's not about being the most charismatic person in the room but about being present, attentive, and genuine in your approach. For some, conversation flows naturally, seamlessly transitioning between topics and leaving behind a string of engaged, smiling individuals. However, for many, small talk can be a daunting task, riddled with uncertainty and nervousness. If you find yourself in the latter category, take heart; small talk is not an innate talent reserved for the chosen few but a skill that can be developed and honed. Learning to excel at small talk starts with understanding its underlying principles. With a bit of practice, patience, and a genuine willingness to engage with others, you can turn small talk from something that might feel awkward or forced into an easy and rewarding part of your interactions.

By mastering this art, we create a more empathetic and connected society and build connections in a world that often feels disconnected or fragmented. It's not about putting on a show; it's about being yourself, being present, and recognising the value in those brief moments of connection that make up the fabric of our social lives.

Embrace this as a chance to learn and grow and you'll find that the journey of engaging in small talk can be a fulfilling and enjoyable skill to master.

Chit-Chat Around the World:
How Different Cultures Do Small Talk

Small talk is a universal phenomenon, a shared human experience that transcends geographical borders. It's a common thread that connects us, regardless of where we come from. But while engaging in casual conversation is found around the world, the way it's conducted, and the topics considered appropriate can vary greatly from one culture to another.

These variations are often deeply rooted in cultural values, social norms, and historical contexts. What might be a casual and friendly inquiry in one culture, could be perceived as intrusive or impolite in another. Similarly, a topic that sparks lively conversation in one part of the world might be considered taboo or sensitive in another. Understanding these differences is not merely a matter of etiquette; it's a reflection of cultural awareness and sensitivity. It's about recognising that the way people communicate, connect, and build relationships is shaped by a complex interplay of cultural factors. Whether it's the emphasis on harmony in

Japanese communication, the value of directness in German conversation, or the warmth and expressiveness of Brazilian interactions, these nuances tell a story about what a culture values and how it sees the world.

For anyone looking to communicate effectively across cultural boundaries, whether in business, during travel, or in personal relationships, being attuned to these differences is essential. It's not just about avoiding misunderstandings or potential offences; it's about building bridges of understanding, showing respect for diverse perspectives, and creating connections that are genuine and meaningful.

In a globalised world, where interactions with people from different cultural backgrounds are increasingly common, the ability to navigate the subtleties of small talk becomes a valuable skill. It's a tool that fosters empathy, boosts social intelligence, and enriches our interactions, making them more nuanced, thoughtful, and genuinely human. By embracing the diversity of small talk and recognising its cultural variations, we open doors to deeper connections and broader understanding.

It's a journey that invites us to see the world through others' eyes, to appreciate the beauty of difference and to find common ground in our shared desire to connect.

Greetings Across Cultures: The Starting Point of Small Talk

Greetings are often the gateway to small talk, the first step in acknowledging someone's presence and initiating a conversation. They serve as the initial touch point in many interactions, setting the tone for the conversation that follows and signalling a willingness to engage. But just as small talk topics can vary across cultures, so can the ways people greet one another. Understanding these variations is not only fascinating but also essential for anyone engaging with different cultures.

In the United States and Canada, the customary greeting often begins with a straightforward "Hello" or "Hi." This is typically succeeded by the question, "How are you?" While this inquiry might seem routine or even rhetorical, it carries with it an underlying warmth and openness. It's an invitation, albeit a casual one, for the other person to share a bit about their day or their feelings. Even if the expected response is often a brief "Good" or "Fine, thanks," the exchange establishes a connection, setting a positive and friendly tone for the conversation that follows.

Other cultures have their unique nuances. For instance, in France, greetings carry with them a blend of tradition and intimacy. Among friends and acquaintances, it's customary to exchange a light kiss on both cheeks. A gesture, known as 'la bise.' However, in more formal settings or when meeting someone for the first time, the French often resort to verbal greetings. A crisp "Bonjour" (Good morning) or "Bonsoir" (Good evening) is extended, accompanied by a handshake. The choice of greeting, be it the familial cheek kiss or the more reserved verbal acknowledgement, provides insight into the nature of the relationship and the context of the meeting, showcasing the French's ability to seamlessly blend tradition with situational appropriateness.

In Japan, the act of bowing, known as 'ojigi,' is deeply rooted in the culture and serves as a primary form of greeting. More than just a physical gesture, a bow embodies the values of respect, humility, and gratitude. It's a silent yet powerful way of communicating one's feelings and intentions. The nuances of the bow are intricate. The depth and duration of the bow can convey different messages. For instance, a slight nod might be suitable for casual interactions, while a deeper, more prolonged bow often signifies a higher level of respect or apology. Such bows are typically reserved for formal occasions, interactions with elders, or situations where one wishes to express deep gratitude or remorse. The subtleties of this gesture highlight the Japanese emphasis on understanding and respecting social hierarchies and the importance of non-verbal communication in their culture.

In India, the term "Namaste" is more than just a casual greeting; it's a gesture steeped in ancient traditions and spiritual significance. The word itself is derived from Sanskrit and can be broken down into 'namas,' meaning 'bow,' and 'te,' meaning 'to you.' Thus, "Namaste" essentially translates to 'I bow to you.' When uttering the word, it's customary to press the palms together, fingers pointing upwards, close to the heart. This gesture, known as 'Anjali Mudra' in yogic traditions, symbolises the meeting of two souls. By doing so, the greeter acknowledges the divine spark within the person they are addressing, suggesting that the essence of both individuals is the same. In a country as diverse as India, where myriad languages and customs coexist, "Namaste" serves as a unifying and universally understood symbol of reverence, humility, and honor.

In Brazil, a country known for its vibrant culture and warm hospitality, greetings are often infused with genuine enthusiasm and affection. Among close friends and family, it's not unusual to be greeted with a tight embrace or a series of cheek kisses, sometimes two or three depending on the region. This tactile approach to greetings reflects the Brazilian emphasis on close personal relationships and their inherent warmth. For more casual interactions or among acquaintances, the laid-back and friendly nature of Brazilians shines through in their choice of greetings. The word "Oi," a simple 'Hi,' is frequently used, showcasing the country's informal and approachable demeanour. Another popular greeting is "Tudo bem?", which translates to 'Is everything good?' It's a casual inquiry into one's well-being and serves as both a greeting and a genuine expression of concern. Whether through physical gestures or cheerful words, Brazilian greetings encapsulate the nation's spirit of camaraderie and joie de vivre.

In Saudi Arabia, the intricacies of greetings are deeply rooted in cultural traditions, societal norms, and religious customs. When men greet each other, especially if they are familiar or of the same age group, it's customary for them to engage in a firm handshake followed by two kisses on the cheek. This gesture is a sign of camaraderie and mutual respect. However, the dynamics shift when it comes to interactions between men and women or even among women themselves. Due to the conservative nature of Saudi society and the emphasis on modesty, greetings between opposite genders, especially if they aren't closely related, tend to be more reserved. A simple nod or a verbal greeting might suffice, avoiding physical contact. Among women, the greetings can vary based on their relationship and familiarity. Close friends or relatives might hug or kiss, while acquaintances might stick to verbal salutations. It's essential to be aware of these nuances, as they reflect the deep-seated values and etiquettes of Saudi Arabian society, ensuring interactions remain respectful and appropriate for the given context.

The African continent, with its vast expanse and diverse cultures, is a treasure trove of unique greetings that mirror its rich heritage. Each region, tribe, and community have its distinct way of acknowledging one another, making every interaction a lesson in history and tradition. For instance, in some West African nations, handshakes can be elaborate affairs, often accompanied by finger snapping. In South Africa, the Zulu greeting "Sawubona," meaning "I see you," goes beyond mere acknowledgement, emphasising recognition and respect for the individual. In East Africa, particularly among the Swahili-speaking populations of Kenya and Tanzania, "Habari" is a common greeting, often followed by inquiries about one's family, health, and work. In Ethiopia, a country with ancient Christian roots, the traditional greeting among the Amhara people involves touching shoulders, known as the "Eskista" greeting. It's a gesture that symbolises friendship and equality.

These instances only scratch the surface of a world teeming with linguistic and cultural richness, yet they showcase the vast array of greetings that span the globe, each echoing distinct cultural values, societal norms, and deep-rooted traditions. From respectful bows to warm kisses, and casual waves, these gestures are more than just routine—they are expressions of identity, connection, and the core of human interaction.

As we explore the world of small talk across cultures, these greetings remind us that even the simplest interactions are rich with meaning and potential. They invite us to approach each conversation with curiosity, openness, and respect, recognising the beauty and complexity of our global tapestry of communication.

Personal Space Across Cultures: Influencing Small Talk in Face-to-Face Interactions

Have you ever noticed the space people maintain between each other while engaging in conversation at a social gathering or waiting in line at a store? It's something we might not think about often, but personal space is a big part of how we communicate. Much like traditional customs or culinary preferences, our sense of personal space can be deeply influenced by our culture.

Personal space is that invisible bubble we carry around with us, a comfort zone that we instinctively maintain. It's a fascinating aspect of human behaviour, one that often operates below our conscious awareness. You might find yourself stepping back if someone stands too close or leaning in if they're too far away. These subtle adjustments are part of a complex dance that helps us navigate social interactions.

But what feels "too close" or "too far" isn't the same for everyone. That's where culture comes into play.

In the United States and Canada, people often prefer a bit more elbow room. If you've ever been to a busy city in North America, you might have noticed that even in a crowded subway, folks try to maintain a little bubble of personal space. In casual conversations, standing an arm's length apart is usually the norm. Get too close, and someone might take a step back! Now, head over to Italy or Brazil, and you'll find a whole different vibe. In these cultures, personal space bubbles are often smaller, and people tend to stand closer together when they talk. A pat on the back or a touch on the arm is a common part of conversation. It's a warm and engaging way to communicate, reflecting a more tactile and close-knit social fabric. In Japan, personal space is often linked to respect and social hierarchy. Standing too close to someone might be seen as impolite, especially if you're talking to someone older or in a higher position. Bowing from a respectful distance is a common greeting, and physical touch is usually minimal. Similarly to greetings, personal space in the Middle East is diverse, particularly in interactions between men and women. Men may often stand closely and even hold hands as a gesture of friendship, while a respectful distance is usually observed between men and women who are not related, to signify respect. In Nordic countries like Finland and Sweden, personal space tends to be larger, reflecting a cultural value on privacy and individuality. Standing too close to someone you don't know well might be seen as intrusive. It's not a sign of coldness but a way to honour each person's personal space and comfort.

Business settings provide another interesting perspective. In a globalised world, understanding cultural differences in personal space can be crucial in professional interactions. Imagine negotiating a deal or building a partnership with someone from a different cultural background. Recognising their comfort zone and adapting your behaviour can be crucial in cultivating trust and effective collaboration.

Technology is also changing how we perceive personal space. With the rise of virtual meetings and social media, we're engaging in new forms of communication that don't have physical boundaries. How does this influence our sense of personal space in face-to-face interactions? It's a question that researchers and social observers are exploring as our world continues to evolve.

So, why does all this matter, especially when it comes to small talk?

Well, understanding these cultural nuances can make our face-to-face interactions smoother and more enjoyable. Imagine you're at an international conference, and you strike up a conversation with someone from a different part of the world. Knowing a bit about their cultural approach to personal space can help you connect more comfortably. If you're chatting with someone from a culture that values close interaction, leaning in and showing engagement through body language can make the conversation feel more genuine. On the other hand, if you're talking to someone from a culture that prefers more distance, respecting that space can show that you're considerate and attentive to their comfort.

In the end, it's all about recognising that our way of doing things isn't the only way. Just as we adapt our language when we learn that someone doesn't speak our native tongue, we can adjust our body language and sense of personal space to connect more meaningfully with others.

Isn't it wonderful how something as simple as standing a little closer or a little farther away can open doors to understanding and friendship? Our world is a beautiful mosaic of traditions and customs, and even in the smallest interactions, we can celebrate and embrace that diversity.

The Global Dance of Small Talk: Navigating Cultural Norms and Taboos

Say you're at an international business event, a friend's wedding or a music festival and you're surrounded by people from all corners of the globe. Eager to engage and connect, you strike up a conversation with someone new. But what do you talk about? What topics are safe to discuss? Determining which topics are universally acceptable and which might be seen as taboo requires a keen awareness. It's a skill we all hone, deciphering the unspoken rules of small talk, and the nuances can be as diverse and vibrant as the cultures we come from.

In many cultures, the topic of family often holds a special place in the hearts of people. Initiating a conversation by asking about family is seen as a gesture of genuine interest and warmth. For instance, in countries such as India or Mexico, where familial bonds are deeply woven into the societal fabric, discussing family can serve as a heart-warming bridge to deeper connections. Here, family isn't just about immediate kin; it's a tapestry of extended relations, ancestral stories, and shared celebrations. Engaging in conversations about family in these regions offers more than just personal insights; it's an invitation to understand the rhythms, values, and traditions that shape daily life. However, the nuances lie in the approach. While the overarching theme of family might be universal, the specifics can be sensitive. Directly asking about someone's marital status or the presence of children might be warmly received in one culture but could be perceived as intrusive in others. In places like Japan or Finland, where there's greater emphasis on maintaining personal boundaries and respecting privacy, such direct questions might be viewed as overly intrusive. In these contexts, it's not just about the question itself, but the intent and manner in which it's posed. It's always wise to be observant and sensitive, ensuring that your conversational approach aligns with the cultural norms and values of the person you're speaking with. This not only prevents potential misunderstandings but also fosters a sense of mutual respect and understanding.

Discussing personal finances can be a tricky terrain. In many Western cultures, such as the United States, it's standard practice to inquire about someone's profession as part of casual conversation. This is often seen as a way to understand a person's interests, background, or daily life. However, crossing over into specifics like salary or personal wealth can be perceived as overstepping, potentially leading to discomfort or perceived rudeness. On the other hand, in certain regions like parts of China, direct questions about income aren't necessarily taboo. Here, such inquiries might be interpreted as a genuine sign of interest or even concern for the individual's well-being. It's a reflection of the cultural differences in how financial matters are perceived and discussed.

Ah, the weather! It's often a safe and neutral topic, especially in places like the United Kingdom, where the weather is famously capricious. Discussing the latest rain shower or unexpected sunny spell is almost a national pastime. It's a way to break the ice without venturing into potentially sensitive areas. But even this seemingly innocuous subject can have cultural nuances. While in many places it's merely a conversational filler, in others, it carries deeper connotations. For instance, in several Middle Eastern countries, where religious and cultural beliefs are deeply intertwined, the weather is often seen as a manifestation of God's will. In such contexts, complaining about the heat or showing dissatisfaction with the weather might be perceived as showing ingratitude for God's blessings. It's a poignant reminder that even the most seemingly neutral topics can be laden with cultural significance. Thus, while the weather remains a reliable conversation starter in many parts of the world, it's always beneficial to approach the topic with an awareness of local customs and beliefs, ensuring our remarks resonate with respect and understanding.

Food, with its rich flavours, aromas, and textures, is a shared pleasure that transcends borders. Discussing favourite dishes, local delicacies, or recent culinary adventures can serve as a delightful bridge in conversations, allowing individuals to bond over shared tastes or introduce each other to new gastronomic experiences. It's a topic that often evokes passion, memories, and even a sense of identity as many cultures are deeply intertwined with their culinary traditions. However, as with any topic, it's essential to approach discussions about food with sensitivity and awareness. Dietary choices and restrictions can be influenced by a myriad of factors, including religious beliefs, cultural practices, personal health, or ethical considerations. For instance, while pork might be a staple in many cuisines, it's prohibited in Islamic and Jewish dietary laws. Similarly, many Indians, particularly Hindus, abstain from beef due to religious beliefs, and a significant number might be vegetarians. Moreover, the rise of various dietary lifestyles and choices, such as veganism, gluten-free, or paleo diets, further underscores the need for mindfulness. What might be a mouth-watering delicacy for one could be a source of discomfort or offence to another.

Politics, with its intricate web of beliefs, policies, and ideologies, often ignites strong emotions and convictions. For many, it's not just about governance but reflects deeper values, aspirations, and visions for society. In some cultures, political discourse is not only accepted but actively encouraged and seen as a vital part of civic engagement and intellectual exchange. For instance, in countries like France, where café culture and intellectual debates have a long-standing tradition, discussing politics can be as common as commenting on the weather. The French often pride themselves on their robust democratic traditions and might engage in spirited discussions about various political ideologies or current events. Similarly, in Greece, the birthplace of democracy, political discourse has historically been a central part of public life, with lively debates taking place in town squares, family gatherings, and local taverns. However, the landscape shifts considerably in other parts of the world. In nations like Thailand or Singapore, where political stability and harmony are highly valued, delving into political discussions, especially those that might be perceived as critical of the government or monarchy, can be sensitive. In such contexts, political discussion is not only a possible cause for differing views but could also have legal implications. Therefore, it is crucial to have a keen understanding of the cultural and political environment when approaching such subjects. While politics offers a wealth of topics for conversation, revealing insights into a country's history, culture, and values, it is important to tread carefully, respectfully, and with an open mindset. Being well-informed and attuned to local subtleties ensures that discussions stay productive and respectful, promoting understanding rather than division.

Religion, for many individuals, extends beyond mere beliefs; it profoundly mirrors their identity, values, and perspective on life. Interlaced with historical, cultural, and personal experiences, religion is a topic that is deeply ingrained and frequently charged with emotion. The way religion is perceived and discussed varies significantly across the globe. For instance, in countries such as India, where spirituality is closely interwoven with daily life, conversations about religious festivals, rituals, and beliefs are often a regular aspect of daily interactions. The country's rich tapestry of diverse religious practices, encompassing a wide array of festivals and traditions, often becomes a focal point of interest and engagement. Conversely, in nations like Sweden or Denmark, which have seen a rise in secularism, religion might be viewed more as a private matter. While discussions about spirituality aren't necessarily taboo, they might not be as commonplace in casual conversations, indicating a wider social trend towards a more personal and private approach to faith. In some Middle Eastern countries, where religion plays a central role in governance and daily life, discussions about faith can be both common and sensitive. While it might be usual to talk about religious practices or teachings, it's crucial to approach such discussions with a deep sense of respect, avoiding topics that might be considered blasphemous or controversial. Moreover, in places with a history of religious conflict or tension, such as Northern Ireland or parts of the Balkans, broaching the subject might unearth deep-seated emotions and memories. In these contexts, it's essential to tread with caution, recognising the historical and personal weight the topic might carry. Ultimately, when discussing religion, it's paramount to approach the subject with empathy, curiosity, and an open mind. By understanding the cultural and personal significance of religious beliefs and practices, one can engage in meaningful and respectful dialogue, enriching one's perspective and fostering mutual understanding.

Gender roles and norms, deeply embedded in the cultural fabric of societies, play a major role in shaping how people interact with each other. These roles, often shaped by historical, religious, and societal factors, dictate what is deemed acceptable behaviour between genders in different situations. For instance, in nations such as Australia, the United States, and numerous regions of Western Europe, gender norms have undergone significant changes, shaped by the influence of feminist movements, shifts in societal perspectives, and progressive policies. In these regions, men and women often interact freely in both professional and social settings. Casual conversations, friendly banter, or even lighthearted teasing between genders are generally accepted and seen as part of the social fabric. However, in more conservative or traditional societies, the dynamics can be quite different. As previously touched on, countries in parts of the Middle East, Asia, or Africa might have stricter boundaries in male-female interactions, especially outside of family circles. These boundaries are often rooted in religious beliefs, traditional values, or societal structures that emphasise modesty and decorum in interactions between genders. In such cultures, what might be perceived as harmless chatter in a Western context could be seen as forward, disrespectful, or even taboo. For example, direct eye contact, physical touch, or certain topics of conversation might be reserved only for close family or same-gender interactions in some cultures. In places like Saudi Arabia or Pakistan, mixed-gender gatherings might have specific protocols and casual conversations between unrelated men and women could be limited. It's also worth noting that these norms can vary widely even within a country, influenced by urban-rural divides, education levels, and individual family values. As such, when interacting in a multicultural setting, it's essential to be observant, respectful, and adaptable. By understanding and respecting these nuances, one can navigate conversations more effectively, ensuring that interactions are both meaningful and appropriate for the cultural context.

Understanding diverse cultural norms and taboos can be challenging, yet it's this very diversity that adds depth to our global landscape. Consider it a journey of understanding, where each interaction is shaped by distinct traditions, values, or lifestyles. At the heart of this journey is empathy, genuine interest, and a readiness to embrace new learning experiences. It's about acknowledging that our worldview is merely one among countless others. By engaging in small talk with an open mind and a keen sense of listening, we pave the way for mutual understanding, one chat at a time.

The Role of Humour in Small Talk Across Cultures

Humour, in its many forms, serves as a universal bridge, drawing people together through shared moments of laughter and light-heartedness. Yet, its application in casual conversations can differ significantly across cultures. Context is everything when it comes to humour. In some cultures, humour is a common way to break the ice. In countries like the United States or the United Kingdom, humour is often used as a tool to ease into conversations. A playful comment about a popular TV show or a humorous observation about a recent trending topic can set a relaxed tone for the interaction. It's a way of saying, 'Let's not take everything too seriously.' In contrast in Japan, humour might be more subtle and situational. Humour tends to be more nuanced. Here, humour isn't always about eliciting a loud laugh; it's about creating a moment of shared recognition, a nod to the intricacies of the situation. This kind of humour requires a keen sense of awareness and often a deeper understanding of cultural references.

Sensitivity to cultural norms is also essential. What's considered humorous in one culture might not translate well into another. For instance, a joke that evokes hearty laughter in Australia might be met with puzzled looks in Germany, where humour often leans towards being more structured, precise, and situational. Similarly, sarcasm, prevalent in British humour, might be misconstrued in cultures unaccustomed to it. Beyond just the style of humour, certain topics that are humorous in one culture might be considered taboo or inappropriate in another. Thus, being attuned to these cultural subtleties not only prevents potential faux pas but also paves the way for more genuine and meaningful interactions. When in doubt, it's always a good strategy to observe and listen first, allowing the cues from others to guide one's approach to humour.

Language and wordplay are foundational elements in the realm of humour. The very essence of a joke or a witty remark often hinges on the clever use of language, puns, or idiomatic expressions that might be deeply rooted in a particular culture's linguistic traditions. Take the

United Kingdom, for instance. British humour is renowned for its dry wit, characterised by understated remarks, irony, and a particular brand of sarcasm. This humour often draws upon the nuances of the English language, employing double entendres, subtle wordplay, and cultural references that might be lost on those unfamiliar with British culture or the intricacies of the language. Moreover, idiomatic expressions, which are phrases whose meanings cannot be deduced from the literal definitions of the words that make them up, can be a goldmine for humour in many cultures. However, they can also be a potential pitfall for those unfamiliar, as their humorous intent can be easily lost in translation. Therefore, for anyone looking to engage in light-hearted small talk across cultures, a deeper dive into the linguistic peculiarities and humour styles of that culture can be immensely beneficial. It not only aids in understanding and appreciating the humour but also ensures that one's attempts at humour resonate as intended.

The social and historical backdrop plays a crucial role in shaping a region's sense of humour. Take South Africa as an example. With its complex history of apartheid and social turmoil, humour frequently serves as a medium to underscore and critique societal matters. Comedians and everyday individuals alike might employ satire or wit to shed light on ongoing challenges or past struggles, using laughter as both a coping mechanism and a form of social commentary. This intertwining of humour with deeper societal narratives not only offers a unique comedic experience but also provides insights into the nation's collective psyche and values. When we, as listeners or participants, discern these underlying themes, it not only enhances our understanding of the joke but also deepens our appreciation of the cultural richness and resilience from which it springs.

In conclusion, humour is more than just a way to make people laugh; it's a reflection of cultural values, social norms, and human connection. By grasping the nuances of humour in small talk across diverse cultures, we can traverse our global society with understanding, reverence, and a sincere appreciation for the multifaceted spectrum of human communication.

A Friendly Guide to Cross-Cultural Chit-Chat: Practical Tips for Engaging in Small Talk

Do Your Homework: Before diving into a conversation, take a moment to learn about the cultural background of the person you're speaking with or the event you're attending. Understanding basic norms and values can go a long way in making your conversation smooth and enjoyable. A quick internet search or a glance at a travel guide can provide valuable insights.

Mind Your Manners: Every culture has its unique etiquette, and being aware of these can help you navigate conversations with grace. Whether it's a respectful bow in Japan or a firm handshake in the United States, these small gestures can make a big impression.

Listen and Learn: Sometimes, the best way to engage is simply to listen. Show genuine interest in the other person's experiences, thoughts, and feelings. Ask open-ended questions and let them guide the conversation. You might learn something new and fascinating!

Be Mindful of Taboos: As we've explored earlier, certain topics might be considered sensitive or inappropriate in some cultures. Steering clear of these areas can help keep the conversation light and pleasant. When in doubt, stick to neutral topics like the weather, food, or popular local activities.

Use Simple Language: If you're speaking with someone whose first language is different from yours, try to use clear and simple language. Avoid idioms or slang that might be confusing. Your effort to communicate clearly will likely be appreciated.

Share Your Culture: Don't be shy about sharing aspects of your own culture. People often enjoy learning about different ways of life, and your personal stories can add a delightful flavour to the conversation.

Respect Personal Space: As we've seen, personal space can vary widely across cultures. Pay attention to body language and adjust your distance accordingly. If someone seems uncomfortable, give them a little more space.

Embrace the Silence: In some cultures, silence is not an awkward pause but a natural part of the conversation. If you find yourself in a moment of quiet, don't rush to fill it. Enjoy the silence and let the conversation flow naturally.

Use Humour Wisely: While humour can be a wonderful way to connect, it can also be culturally specific. If you choose to add a touch of humour, be mindful of how it might be received. A smile, however, is a universal sign of friendliness.

Be Yourself: Finally, remember to be yourself. Authenticity shines through, and people often respond positively to genuine interest and kindness.

Embarking on the adventure of cross-cultural small talk is like exploring a new landscape, filled with unique traditions, customs, and ways of thinking. It's an opportunity to grow, learn, and connect on a human level. So next time you find yourself face-to-face with someone from a different culture, take a deep breath, smile, and dive into the conversation. With these practical tips in your back pocket, you'll be well-equipped to enjoy the dance of small talk, wherever your journey takes you.

Happy chatting!

Digital Small Talk: Mastering Communication in the Age of Social Media and Texting

Step into the digital era, where conversations have evolved from local gatherings and community spaces to global platforms and digital interfaces. The sharing of a funny meme or an insightful comment on social media showcases the modern adaptation of small talk in our connected world.

In previous generations, small talk thrived on face-to-face interactions. Neighbours would engage in conversation over the garden fence, and colleagues would discuss the latest news by the water cooler. Today, the landscape of casual conversation has expanded, thanks to the wonders of technology. The world has become a vast virtual realm, where connections are made and conversations are had, not just across the street but across continents. This shift is not merely about the evolution of communication tools, but it also embodies a fresh approach to how individuals connect, share, and engage with one another. It underscores the adaptability and innovation of human connections in an ever-changing world.

Platforms like Facebook, Twitter, and Instagram have transformed into digital hubs for interaction, sharing, and active engagement. These sites have globalised small talk, where even a simple "like" or emoji can initiate a connection. From sharing moments of happiness to conveying grief, and yes, even posting beloved cat videos, these platforms facilitate real-time interaction across the world. Texting, especially through platforms like WhatsApp and group chats, has dramatically transformed communication. Gone are the days when arranging an outing required a phone call. Nowadays, a quick text, often accompanied by a smiley face can coordinate plans. This mode of communication offers a convenient way to stay connected, share glimpses of daily life, and convey emotions, all through a few taps on a phone.

But this digital evolution comes with its own set of hurdles. The subtleties of tone, body language, and facial expressions that we rely on in face-to-face interactions can get lost in translation online. Ever sent a text and worried it might be taken the wrong way? You're not alone! Emojis and GIFs have emerged as tools to bridge this gap, adding flavour and personality to digital chats. They serve as the online equivalents of a smile, a frown, or a wink, helping to convey emotions and intentions in a way that plain text might not capture.

The etiquette of digital small talk is also a fascinating landscape to navigate. When is it appropriate to use a casual tone in an email? How long should you wait before following up on a text? These are the new rules of engagement we're all learning together. And let's not forget the incredible power of connection that digital small talk offers. It's a way to stay close to loved ones far away, to reconnect with old friends, and to discover new ones. It's a world where a shared interest in gardening, vintage cars or crocheting can spark friendships that transcend geographical boundaries.

So, dear reader, as we embrace this brave new world of digital small talk, let's celebrate the connections, the creativity, and the endless possibilities it offers. Let's also be mindful of the nuances, the etiquette, and the human touch that makes small talk, whether online or offline, a vital part of our social fabric. In the end, whether it's tweeting, texting, or engaging in a direct conversation, the essence of communication remains the same. It's about forging a bond and sharing a moment. It's a timeless gesture that says, "I'm present, and I value this interaction."

Navigating the Social Seas: Adapting Small Talk to Different Social Media Platforms

Each platform has its own rhythm, style, and unwritten rules. Adapting to these nuances isn't just about fitting in; it's about maximizing the potential of each interaction. From the cordial exchanges on Facebook to the rapid-fire conversations on Twitter, to the visually captivating dialogues on Instagram, the spectrum of online communication is rich and varied. Understanding how each platform provides its distinct avenue for small talk can enhance communication and transform basic exchanges into impactful connections.

Facebook: Community Conversations. Facebook, particularly within its community groups, acts as a social hub where friends, family, and likeminded individuals connect by sharing updates, photos, and news. Interactions in these groups and on general Facebook feeds are typically friendly and personal, with comments and reactions fuelling the dialogue. Maintaining respect and positivity is crucial for nurturing a communal atmosphere.

Twitter: Brevity Meets Brilliance. Twitter thrives on swift and succinct interactions. Whether you're diving into a trending conversation or sharing a brief thought, the platform values short, sharp content. Its character constraint nudges users to be both concise and captivating.

Instagram: A Picture's Worth a Thousand Words. On Instagram, images take centre stage, and captions add context and creativity. Interaction revolves around visual content, with likes, comments, and emojis enhancing the connection. It's a platform where visual expression thrives.

LinkedIn: Professional Networking. LinkedIn emphasizes professional connections and career-related content. Interaction here is more formal, focusing on industry insights, job achievements, and networking opportunities. A polished and professional approach is appreciated.

TikTok: Creativity in Motion. TikTok celebrates creativity, fun, and entertainment. Engagement on this platform often involves participating in challenges, commenting on trending videos, or creating unique content. It's a space that encourages joy and creative expression.

Reddit: Interest-Based Communities. Reddit offers a wide array of interest-based communities known as subreddits. Engagement here involves asking questions, sharing insights, and participating in discussions related to specific interests. Adhering to community guidelines is essential for positive interaction.

WhatsApp and Messenger: Personal Connections. WhatsApp and Messenger facilitate private and group conversations, often among friends and family. Interaction here is casual and intimate, suitable for sharing personal updates, planning events, or simply checking in.

Understanding the unique characteristics of each social media platform can enhance the experience of engaging in small talk online. By doing so, users can participate in meaningful and enjoyable interactions that reflect the diverse and dynamic world of social media.

Navigating the Norms and Etiquette of Digital Communication

In today's digital era, where a significant portion of our interactions happen through screens and keyboards, grasping the nuances and etiquette of online interactions is not just beneficial; it's essential. From the brief interactions on social media to the more formal discussions in professional emails, there is a distinct set of rules that govern our online conversations.

The timing of responses in digital interactions carries subtle yet significant implications. In professional or urgent contexts, a prompt reply can convey attentiveness and respect, indicating that the recipient prioritizes the exchange and values the communication. On the other hand, a prolonged delay might be perceived as disinterest, neglect, or even rudeness, which could potentially strain the relationship. However, these interpretations are not universal and can vary widely depending on several factors. The context of the conversation, whether casual or formal, can influence expectations. A delayed response to a business inquiry might be seen as unprofessional, while the same delay in responding to a friend's social media post might go unnoticed. The platform itself can also set the tone. Instant messaging apps may create an expectation for rapid responses, while email might allow for more time. The relationship between the communicators further complicates the matter. Close friends might have an understanding that allows for slower responses, while new or professional connections might expect more promptness. In an era where digital messages can be sent and received in mere seconds, grasping these subtleties and setting clear expectations can be key for fostering positive and respectful exchanges. It's a delicate balance of timing, demanding mindfulness, understanding, and at times, explicit communication about one's boundaries and anticipations.

Emojis, those small yet expressive symbols, have become like a second language for many of us, enriching our online conversations with flair, sentiment, and individuality. They act as a visual shorthand, capturing emotions and nuances that might be difficult to express through text alone. A smiley face can add warmth and friendliness to a message, while a thumbs-up can signal agreement or approval, and a heart can express affection or support. They can be real communication helpers, especially when words fall short. However, the use of emojis is not without its complexities. It should be tailored to the context and audience to ensure that the intended message is conveyed. In a professional email or formal correspondence, excessive emojis might seem unprofessional or even inappropriate. They might dilute the seriousness of the message or create confusion. On the other hand, in a friendly chat or social media post, emojis can enhance connection and understanding. They can add humour, soften a statement, or emphasize a point. They allow for a more casual and expressive form of communication that can make digital interactions feel more personal and engaging. Understanding when and how to use emojis is an essential aspect of digital literacy. It's about recognizing the tone and purpose of the communication and choosing emojis that enhance rather than detract from the message. In this way, emojis become more than just decorative symbols; they serve as instruments that amplify our digital conversations, blending written text with genuine sentiment. And given the prevalence of screen-based interactions in our era, that's something to smile about – emoji smile, of course!

The choice of language plays a crucial role in digital communication, and finding the right tone can make all the difference. In various online interactions, the choice of words, phrases, and even punctuation can set the tone for the entire conversation. Formal language, complete with proper grammar and a more structured style, might be expected in a business setting, such as a professional email or a corporate social media account. This approach conveys respect and seriousness, aligning with traditional business etiquette. Conversely, casual and colloquial expressions might be more suitable for social media posts, personal texts, or online forums. This relaxed style allows for a more personal connection, fostering a sense of community and shared understanding. Emoticons, abbreviations, and informal language can make the conversation feel more like a chat between friends. Being mindful of the audience and the platform is key to guiding the choice of language. Understanding who you're speaking to and what the expectations might be ensures that the message is received as intended. It's about striking the right balance between formality and informality, recognizing the context, and choosing words that resonate with the audience.

In the fast-paced digital age of today, where interactions occur in an instant, abbreviations and digital linguistic tools have become indispensable. From "LOL" (Laughing Out Loud) to "WYD" (What You Doing), these acronyms have become part of our digital dialogue. They add personality and emotion to our conversations, turning plain text into something livelier and engaging. A well-placed "OMG" (Oh My Gosh) can convey surprise, while a simple "TTYL" (Talk To You Later) sends a friendly farewell. Hashtags, too, have evolved into a language tool of their own. What began as a way to categorize content on social media has turned into a form of expression. Using a hashtag like #TravelTueday connects us to broader conversations and shared experiences, creating a sense of community.

But with all these digital tools comes the need for awareness and understanding. Digital shorthand is often more suited to informal conversations and settings. While a well-timed "LMAO" in a friendly chat can lighten the mood, using too many acronyms in a professional setting might seem out of place. It's essential to recognize when these playful expressions fit the context, and when they might be best left for more casual interactions. Also, as new acronyms and expressions emerge all the time, we cannot forget that not everyone speaks this digital shorthand fluently. While these tools can connect us, they can also create confusion if we're not mindful of our audience. It's a delicate balance between embracing the convenience and creativity of digital language and ensuring clear communication.

Keep it concise, especially when texting. Texting is meant for quick, informal communication, and one of its greatest strengths is its ability to convey thoughts briefly and efficiently. When engaging in small talk through texting, it's essential to keep your messages brief and to the point. Lengthy paragraphs might be overwhelming and can lose the reader's interest. Imagine receiving a text that looks more like a novel; it might be daunting to even start reading. Consider breaking up your thoughts into smaller, digestible chunks. If you have several points to make, you might send them as separate messages rather than one long paragraph. This approach can make the conversation feel more dynamic and interactive. Also, be mindful of the recipient's time and attention. People often check texts on the go, during breaks, or in between tasks. A concise message respects their time and makes it easier for them to engage with you. However, conciseness shouldn't come at the expense of clarity. Make sure your message is clear and doesn't leave the recipient guessing your intentions. If something requires more explanation, consider whether texting is the right medium or if a phone call or face-to-face conversation might be more appropriate.

Privacy and security considerations take on special importance. Engaging in conversations online is not just about sharing thoughts and emotions; it's also about being mindful of the information we reveal and the platforms we use. While it's natural to want to connect and share with others, it's wise to remember that digital spaces are not always as private as they may seem. A casual mention of a weekend plan or a favourite hangout spot might seem harmless, but in the wrong hands, such information could be misused. Security considerations extend to the platforms and tools we use for digital communication. Ensuring that our devices are protected with up-to-date security measures and that we're using trusted platforms can go a long way in safeguarding our online interactions. Moreover, being aware of the privacy settings on social media sites and understanding who can see our posts and comments can help us maintain control over our digital footprint. It's about finding the balance between connecting with others and protecting our privacy. In the end, the principles that guide our face-to-face small talk – trust, respect, and discretion – are equally vital in the digital world. By being mindful of privacy and security considerations, we can enjoy the benefits of digital small talk without compromising our safety and confidentiality.

The Importance of Balancing Digital Communication with Face-to-Face Interactions

While digital communication offers speed and convenience, face-to-face interactions provide depth and richness that can't be replicated through a screen. The nuances of body language, facial expressions, and tone of voice add layers of meaning and connection that digital communication might miss. That's not to say that digital communication doesn't have its place. It's a fantastic tool for maintaining connections, especially with those far away. But it should complement, not replace, face-to-face interactions. Relying solely on digital communication can lead to a comfort zone where the nuances of in-person conversation are lost.

Striking the right balance between digital communication and face-to-face interactions is about recognizing the strengths and limitations of each. It's about choosing the right tool for the right moment, ensuring that our connections remain vibrant, authentic, and fulfilling in both the digital and physical worlds.

Tips for Engaging in Small Talk Online, Without Losing the Personal Touch

1. Know Your Platform: Adjust your communication style to fit the unique culture of platforms like LinkedIn, Facebook, or Instagram. Since every platform comes with its distinct norms and user expectations, tailoring your approach ensures a meaningful experience and effective engagement with your audience.

2. Use Emojis Wisely: Utilize emojis to add a touch of warmth and character into your digital conversations but do so judiciously. While these symbols can enhance the tone of a message and make it more relatable, excessive use might undermine its gravity or come off as unprofessional. Moreover, always be mindful of the context. Being attuned with your audience and the platform will guide you in striking the right balance.

3. Mind Your Tone: Be mindful of your wording, as tone can be tricky to convey online. The words you choose and the way you structure your sentences play a pivotal role in conveying your intended message. Remember, what's clear to you might be ambiguous to someone else, so always strive for clarity and kindness in your online interactions.

4. Respect Privacy: Keep personal or sensitive topics for more secure channels of communication. Topics that involve financial details, confidential information, or deeply personal stories are best reserved for encrypted messaging apps, direct phone calls, or face-to-face conversations. Always prioritize your safety and the confidentiality of the information you're sharing.

5. Keep It Brief: Keep your communication concise and engaging. Lengthy messages or posts can overwhelm or disengage your audience. By keeping your communication brief, you ensure that your main points are easily digestible and memorable.

6. Respond Timely: Try to respond promptly to show interest. If a comprehensive response will take time, a brief acknowledgement that you've received the message and will revert soon can be a considerate gesture. In an age of instant communication, being responsive can set you apart and strengthen your relationships, both personally and professionally.

7. Stay Authentic: Be yourself and let your genuine interest in others shine through. Authenticity fosters trust, and when people sense that you're genuine, they're more likely to open up and connect on a deeper level.

8. Balance with Face-to-Face Communication: Don't get too comfortable relying solely on digital communication. It's essential to balance online small talk with face-to-face interactions to main-

tain well-rounded communication skills. The subtleties of in-person communication adds depth to our connections and should not be overlooked.

Finding Your Voice:

For the Shy, Introverted &

Socially Awkward

In the colourful and complex realm of human personalities, we often come across terms like 'shy', 'introverted', and 'socially awkward'. While they might seem interchangeable to some, they each represent distinct facets of an individual's social behaviour. Understanding these differences can shed light on the unique challenges and strengths each trait brings to social interactions.

Shyness: At its core, shyness is a feeling of apprehension or anxiety in social situations. Those who are shy might fear judgment or negative evaluation by others. This can lead to a reluctance to engage in social interactions, not necessarily because they dislike the company, but because of the anxiety it might provoke. It's worth noting that a shy individual might very much desire social connections but feels held back by their nervousness.

Introversion: Introversion, on the other hand, is more about where an individual draws their energy. Introverts tend to feel more energized and at ease in solitary or low-stimulus environments. They might prefer a quiet evening in watching a film or reading a book over an event or large gathering. Not necessarily due to anxiety, but because they genuinely enjoy solitude or small group interactions. It's a natural inclination rather than a reaction to fear.

Social Awkwardness: Social awkwardness is characterized by challenges in navigating social norms. An individual might not pick up on social cues, leading to misunderstandings or misinterpretations. It's not about comfort or energy source, as with shyness or introversion, but rather a difficulty in understanding or adhering to the unwritten rules of social engagement.

Each of these traits can impact social interactions in different ways:

- A shy person, for example, might avoid attending a social gathering due to the anxiety it induces, even if they genuinely wish to be part of it. Their reluctance isn't a sign of disinterest but rather a response to the discomfort they feel in unfamiliar social settings.

- In contrast, an introverted individual might attend the same gathering but prefer to engage in one-on-one conversations. They often find solace in deeper, more intimate discussions rather than mingling with a large group.

- Meanwhile, someone who is socially awkward might attend the gathering but struggle with the dynamics of the conversation. They may speak out of turn, misinterpret a joke, or find it challenging to follow engagement. While this may appear clumsy or out of place, it's essential to recognize that it's not a lack of desire to connect but rather a different way of interpreting social cues.

Shy, introverted, and socially awkward individuals often possess unique strengths that can enrich social interactions in ways that might not be immediately apparent. While these traits may sometimes be perceived as hindrances, they can also be sources of valuable qualities.

Shy individuals, for instance, may be hesitant to engage in large group conversations, but this reticence often translates into a thoughtful and attentive presence. Their tendency to observe rather than dominate a conversation can make them excellent listeners. They often provide a supportive and understanding ear, allowing others to express themselves freely. This quality can foster deeper connections and more meaningful interactions.

Introverted people, while perhaps preferring one-on-one conversations or smaller group settings, often excel in creating intimate and thoughtful dialogues. Their preference for depth over breadth in conversation leads to engaging and substantial discussions. They are likely to invest time and energy into understanding others' perspectives and feelings, leading to a more empathetic and compassionate connection. Their ability to focus on the individual and delve into profound topics can turn a casual chat into a memorable and enriching experience.

Socially awkward individuals, despite sometimes struggling with social norms and cues, often bring a unique and refreshing perspective to social interactions. Their unconventional approach to conversation can lead to creative and out-of-the-box thinking. While they might occasionally misstep in terms of social etiquette, their genuine and unfiltered approach can be endearing and provide a break from predictable social scripts. Furthermore, socially awkward individuals often develop resilience and a keen awareness of others' feelings, as they work to navigate social situations. This can translate into a heightened sensitivity to others' needs and a willingness to adapt and learn.

In recognizing these strengths, we can see that shy, introverted, and socially awkward individuals contribute significantly to the diversity and richness of social interactions. They remind us that there is no one-size-fits-all approach to communication and that different personalities bring different gifts to the table. By valuing and embracing these unique qualities, we can foster a more inclusive and empathetic social environment, where everyone's contributions are acknowledged and celebrated.

In a society that often celebrates extroversion, embracing one's unique personality, whether introverted, shy, or socially awkward, can be a powerful act of self-acceptance. Conforming to societal expectations and attempting to fit into an extroverted mould can lead to discomfort, a lack of fulfilment and inauthenticity. By recognizing and honouring individual social behaviours, people can engage more genuinely and foster connections that value diverse communication styles. Moreover, understanding that introversion, shyness, or social awkwardness are not flaws but simply different ways of engaging with the world can lead to a more fulfilling and contented life. It allows individuals to find their own path to social engagement, paths that honour their true selves, and contribute positively to the diverse tapestry of human interaction.

Overcoming the Fear of Judgment

The fear of being judged can be a significant barrier for those who identify as shy or socially awkward. This concern often stems from a heightened sensitivity to how others perceive them, and it can hinder social interactions and personal growth. People with these tendencies might scrutinize their every word and deed, fearing that others might misinterpret or criticize them. This anxiety can result in evading social settings, missing out on opportunities, and feeling isolated. Nonetheless, there are strategies available to help individuals navigate this fear and participate more confidently in social environments.

One approach is to recognize that the fear of judgment is a universal sentiment and is not specifically unique to shy or socially awkward individuals. Nearly everyone has felt the weight of others' opinions at some point. Recognizing this as a collective experience can provide solace and diminish feelings of isolation. It's essential to remember that everyone has their insecurities, and often, people are more preoccupied with their own concerns than with critiquing others. Acknowledging that it's natural to occasionally feel self-conscious can take the pressure off and make social interactions feel more manageable.

Another approach is to practice self-compassion and counteract negative self-perceptions. By being kind to oneself and acknowledging that it's okay to be imperfect can alleviate self-imposed pressures. Embracing imperfections and understanding that making mistakes is a natural part of human interaction can foster a more forgiving attitude towards oneself and individuals can begin to feel more at ease in social situations. Additionally, substituting self-critical thoughts with more constructive and balanced ones can nurture a healthier self-view. Remembering to be gentle with oneself and recognizing that everyone has their own set of challenges can be very liberating.

Building social skills through practice and gradual exposure to social situations can also be beneficial. Starting with smaller, less intimidating settings and gradually working up to more challenging environments can build confidence and resilience. This approach creates a sense of accomplishment and reduces anxiety. Joining social groups that align with personal interests or seeking support from a therapist can provide a safe space to practice and grow. At times when the fear of judgment can be overwhelming, seeking professional assistance or joining groups focused on social anxiety can provide personalized strategies and encouragement.

Finally, focusing on the present moment and engaging in active listening can shift the focus away from self-critique towards authentic engagement. By concentrating on the conversation and the individual they're conversing with, rather than dwelling on personal fears and insecurities, individuals can create deeper and more fulfilling exchanges.

In conclusion, while the fear of being judged can be a daunting obstacle, it doesn't have to define or limit social experiences. With understanding, self-compassion, practice, and a focus on connection, individuals can move beyond this fear and enrich their social lives. It's a journey that may require time and effort, but the rewards of deeper connections and personal growth are well worth the investment.

Building Social Confidence: Practices to Enhance Communication and Connection

1. Start Small: If social situations feel overwhelming, it's often beneficial to start with small, manageable interactions. Engaging in simple exchanges, such as striking up a conversation with a neighbour, complimenting a stranger's outfit, or engaging in small talk with a cashier, can serve as stepping stones. These brief and low-pressure interactions can gradually build confidence and social skills, laying the groundwork for more complex social engagements.

2. Practice Active Listening: Focus on truly hearing and understanding what others are saying. Nod, make eye contact, and ask follow-up questions to show that you're engaged. By listening attentively, you cultivate richer relationships and enhance the quality of conversations for all participants involved.

3. Navigating Comfort Zones: Identifying social environments and situations where one feels most comfortable and authentic is a key strategy in building social confidence. It's about recognizing individual preferences and gravitating towards environments or groups that align well. For example, those with a passion for art might gravitate towards gallery openings or art workshops. On the other hand, individuals who value a quieter ambience might opt for smaller, more intimate gatherings rather than bustling events. By choosing environments that resonate with individual interests and comfort levels, people can engage more authentically and enjoyably. This alignment not only enhances the quality of social interactions but also fosters a sense of belonging and

connection, making social experiences more rewarding and less stressful.

4. Role-Playing: Practice makes perfect, and role-playing with a friend or family member can be a fun way to rehearse social interactions. Choose different scenarios and take turns playing different roles. This exercise can help you anticipate potential conversations and develop responses in a low-pressure environment.

5. Establish Social Goals: Break your social development into manageable milestones. Begin with simpler tasks, like making a point to comment on a colleague's idea during meetings and build from there. As your confidence and comfort grow, progressively increase the challenge.

6. Mindfulness Practices and Deep Breathing: When anxiety poses a challenge to social engagement, utilizing mindfulness routines and focused breathing can effectively soothe apprehensions. By focusing on your breath and grounding yourself in the present moment, you can create a sense of tranquillity and control. This technique aids in silencing the mind, diminishing the inner noise that can amplify anxious feelings. When you approach conversations with a serene and receptive mindset, you'll often discover that dialogues progress more smoothly and connections with others feel more genuine.

7. Pause and Reflect: After social interactions, take a moment to reflect on what went well and what could be improved. Learning from each experience, whether positive or negative, can lead to continuous growth and development.

8. Seek Professional Help if Needed: If social challenges persist or seem too overwhelming to tackle alone, turning to professionals can be a game-changer. Therapists or counsellors with expertise in social interactions not only offer a safe space to discuss and

dissect these challenges but also provide tailored advice, coping techniques, and actionable strategies. They can help individuals understand the root causes of their social anxieties and guide them towards more confident and fulfilling social engagements.

9. Embrace Imperfection: Remember, nobody is perfect, and social interactions don't have to be flawless to be meaningful and enjoyable. Embrace imperfection, be yourself, and focus on genuine connection rather than performance.

10. Prioritizing Self-Care: Taking time to rejuvenate is essential for sustaining a balanced social life, particularly for introverts or people who might feel drained by prolonged social engagements. By recognizing personal limits and allowing time for solitude or engaging in preferred hobbies, introverts can replenish their energy. This self-aware approach ensures that when they do engage in social activities, they do so with full presence, allowing individuals to thrive in both personal and communal spaces.

11. Celebrate Small Victories: Recognizing and applauding even the smallest strides is essential in the journey towards overcoming shyness or social awkwardness. This process isn't about making giant leaps but rather acknowledging and appreciating every little step taken, as each achievement is a building block towards greater confidence. By focusing on progress rather than perfection, individuals can create a positive feedback loop that encourages further growth.

The Brain's Role in Human Connection and Social Interaction

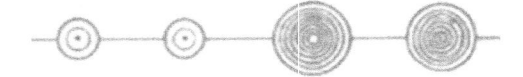

Human beings are inherently social creatures. From the earliest days of our existence, we have relied on community for survival, collaboration, and companionship. This inclination towards socialization isn't just a cultural or societal construct; it's deeply embedded within our DNA. Our brains, with their complex neural pathways, are intricately designed to seek, interpret, and thrive on social interactions and connections. Our evolutionary history underscores the importance of social bonds. Early humans who formed strong social ties had better chances of survival, as they could collaborate in hunting, gathering, and protection. Over time, this need for social connection became an integral part of our evolutionary blueprint. In modern times, while we may not face the same survival challenges as our ancestors, the underlying need for connection remains as potent as ever.

Neuroscientific research has delved deeply into the effects of social interactions on our brain, revealing fascinating insights into our inherent need for connection. When we engage in social interactions, various regions of our brain become activated. For instance, the amygdala. Often referred to as the brain's "emotion centre," plays a pivotal role in processing social emotions like fear, trust and empathy. Located deep within the temporal lobe, when we connect with others, this region helps us interpret and respond to the emotional cues of those around us. It's especially attuned to evaluating facial expressions and emotional reactions, a primary mode of non-verbal communication. The prefrontal cortex, on the other hand, is involved in higher cognitive functions such as decision-making and social cognition. It helps us interpret social cues and predict others' intentions, playing a vital role in our ability to navigate complex social situations. Together, these regions form a dynamic network that enables us to engage in meaningful social interactions. They allow us to connect with others on an emotional level, understand their perspectives, and respond appropriately.

The Love Hormone

Oxytocin, often referred to as the "love hormone" or "social bonding hormone," plays a significant role in human relationships. This fascinating chemical, generated in the brain's hypothalamus and released by the pituitary gland, is a cornerstone of our emotional and social lives. It's responsible for that warm, fuzzy feeling we get when we're close to someone we like or care about. Often released during positive social experiences, such as a comforting touch or a heartfelt conversation, it serves as a bridge, encouraging understanding and deepening ties between people.

Oxytocin plays a role in various aspects of our social lives, from the bond between a mother and her new-born child to the trust between friends and teammates. It's thought to amplify our ability to empathize, helping us better understand and resonate with the feelings and desires of others. In romantic relationships, oxytocin adds a special spark. It increases sensations of intimacy and warmth, making moments spent with a loved one even more memorable. It adds to the captivating magic that makes falling in love such an extraordinary and unforgettable journey.

In social scenarios particularly, oxytocin also has a calming effect. It aids in reducing anxiety and stress, encouraging individuals to engage and turn potentially awkward moments into opportunities for connection. In tough situations, such as disputes or misunderstandings, the presence of oxytocin can promote reconciliation and forgiveness, underscoring its significance in sustaining enduring relationships.

In essence, oxytocin serves as nature's way of ensuring that we, as social beings, remain interconnected and supportive of one another. It's a testament to the profound importance of relationships in our lives, both for our emotional well-being and for the survival and success of our species. It's a remarkable aspect of our human biology.

The Feel-Good Hormone

Spending time with friends isn't just about having fun or passing time; it's a deep-seated human necessity that triggers a reward system in our brain. When we engage in social interactions with friends, our brain releases neurotransmitters like dopamine, often referred to as the "feel-good" hormone.

Dopamine is part of the brain's reward circuitry and is pivotal in how we experience pleasure, motivation and satisfaction. This chemical messenger is intricately linked to how we perceive and react to rewarding stimuli. When we enjoy moments with friends, be it over a shared meal, laughing at a joke, or immersing ourselves in a mutual hobby, our brain interprets these moments as positive and releases dopamine in response. It's a beautifully orchestrated feedback loop that reinforces our desire to seek out such pleasurable experiences again all whilst strengthening our bond with others.

The activation of this reward system is not just about feeling good in the moment; it has long-term benefits for our mental and emotional well-being. Numerous studies have highlighted the myriad benefits of social connections from increased mood and happiness to reduced stress. Moreover, there's compelling evidence to suggest that individuals with robust social networks tend to live longer, healthier lives. They have a lower risk of chronic diseases, mental health disorders, and even cognitive decline as they age. This can be attributed, in part, to the protective effects of positive social interactions on our physiological systems, from bolstering our immune function to regulating our stress hormones.

In an era where the hustle of daily life and busy schedules can sometimes isolate us, understanding the neurological basis of social connections emphasizes the importance of prioritizing time with loved ones. So, the next time you're debating whether to catch up with a friend or go on that coffee date, remember that it's not just good for the soul; it's good for the brain too!

Loneliness and Our Brain: The Neurological and Mental Health Implications

Loneliness is not just an emotional state; it can have serious implications for both the brain and mental health. While occasional feelings of solitude can provide opportunities for introspection and self-discovery, chronic loneliness can have detrimental effects on our neurological well-being.

Loneliness can lead to alterations in the balance of neurotransmitters in the brain. For instance, persistent feelings of isolation can reduce levels of serotonin, a neurotransmitter associated with happiness and well-being, potentially leading to mood disorders such as depression. The lack of social connections can create a self-perpetuating loop: loneliness can trigger depression, which in turn can further isolate the individual. Experiencing loneliness can trigger the body's stress mechanisms. When sustained, this activation can result in increased levels of the stress hormone, cortisol. High cortisol levels are associated with various health concerns, from anxiety and depression to digestive issues, obesity, and sleep disruptions.

Extended periods of loneliness can influence the structure and operation of brain areas related to social cognition and emotional processing. With fewer social interactions, these regions might receive less stimulation, which could alter their connectivity and functionality. Some studies suggest that people who consistently feel lonely might face an increased risk of cognitive decline as they age. Engaging in social interactions is vital for maintaining our cognitive sharpness, and a deficiency in such interactions can hasten the decline associated with ageing.

In conclusion, while loneliness is a complex and multifaceted emotion, its implications for our brain and mental health are undeniable. Recognizing the profound effects of loneliness highlights the importance of seeking connections, whether through social activities, therapy, or community involvement. Ensuring we maintain genuine human connections is more vital than ever for our neurological and emotional well-being.

Bridging Brain and Behaviour

Diving into the brain's intricate mechanisms during social scenarios isn't just a captivating exploration of neuroscience; it's directly applicable to our daily interactions. By recognizing that our brains are wired to connect and that certain hormones facilitate bonding, we can approach social interactions with a more informed perspective.

It's empowering to know that our brains are dynamic entities, continuously evolving and adapting. They're not just hardwired with fixed capabilities but can be trained and refined over time. Social skills, much like any other skill, can be cultivated and improved upon. By actively engaging in social situations, even if initially uncomfortable, helps the brain develop pathways to become more adept at socializing. Just like mastering a new language or musical instrument; with practice and persistence, proficiency grows. This realisation can be a beacon of hope for those who feel challenged in social settings, offering encouragement to participate and hone their skills in fear of permanent failure.

In a nutshell, understanding the "brain stuff" demystifies the complex world of human interactions. It offers both a scientific foundation and a guide to personal growth in social skills, ensuring our interactions are more fulfilling and meaningful. This harmonious blend of science and human experience illuminates the path to richer, more rewarding human connections.

PART 2

The Good, The Bad & The Gabby: Unpacking What Makes a Good (Or Not So Good) Communicator

Good communication is more than just stringing words together; it's an art that requires thoughtfulness, precision, and understanding. In any setting, be it a personal chat, a business discussion, or delivering a public speech, the ability to communicate effectively can be the key factor that determines whether the outcome is clarity and consensus or misunderstanding and disagreement.

Clear communication is about expressing thoughts and ideas in a way that is easily understood. It involves choosing the right words, constructing sentences logically, and avoiding ambiguity. Additionally, good communicators are adaptable, understanding the need to tailor their communication style and method to suit the specific context and audience. Such flexibility in communication is crucial for successful exchanges, emphasising that techniques effective in one scenario might not be suitable in another. Thus, you must be willing to be flexible and responsive to the needs of the moment.

Clarity is a cornerstone of good communication. The ability to convey a message requires an understanding of the audience's background and needs, ensuring that the message is presented at a level they can comprehend. It's about making complex ideas accessible and digestible without diminishing their essence.

Being concise means conveying a message in as few words as necessary without losing the essence of what's being said. It's about being direct and to the point, eliminating unnecessary words and redundancies. Conciseness shows respect for the listener's time and keeps their attention focused on the core message. It's not about being curt or abrupt but about being efficient and thoughtful in word choice.

Effective communication is a reciprocal process that requires an awareness of and respect for the listener. This means actively listening, showing empathy, and acknowledging the listener's feelings and perspectives. It involves being open to feedback and responsive to questions. Respect also means being mindful of cultural differences, avoiding offensive language, and maintaining a tone that is appropriate to the context and relationship.

Beyond words, good communication also involves non-verbal cues such as body language, facial expressions, and tone of voice. These elements can reinforce or contradict the spoken message, so being aware of them and using them intentionally can enhance communication.

Trust is also foundational to effective communication. Being honest, transparent, and consistent in communication builds trust and credibility. It means being true to one's word and following through on commitments.

As you can see, good communication is multifaceted. It's a skill that can be developed and refined through practice and awareness. Whether in personal relationships, professional settings, or community engagements, effective communication is a vital tool for connecting with others, resolving conflicts, and building a shared understanding. It's not just simply about talking; it's about connecting.

Communication Pitfalls: What Not to Do

Communication is a delicate art. It requires a balance of speaking and listening, understanding and expressing, as well as patience and observation. All while manoeuvring through the intricacies of human emotions and perceptions. Even when we approach conversations with the best intentions, it's easy to stumble. These missteps, often born from habits or defence mechanisms, can unintentionally create barriers in our interactions. Whether it's overlooking a non-verbal signal, an unintended tone, or simply the challenge of articulating complex thoughts or ideas, these obstacles can disrupt the flow and harmony of our conversations.

Recognizing and understanding these challenges is the first step towards more effective and empathetic communication. Here are some common mistakes to be mindful of:

Interrupting: Cutting someone off before they've had the chance to complete their thought is more than just a conversational faux pas. It can signal impatience, a lack of interest, or even disrespect. This disruption not only breaks the rhythm of a conversation but can also result in missed information or skewed interpretations. By not allowing the other person to finish, we risk not fully understanding their perspective, which can lead to further miscommunication down the line.

Not Listening: The essence of genuine communication lies in the act of active listening. When we fail to truly tune into what someone is saying, we miss out on the nuances and emotions embedded in their words. This can result in misconceptions and a diminished sense of connection between individuals. Feeling unheard can also create feelings of frustration or insignificance, straying from the intended goal of the conversation.

Being Overly Verbose: Sometimes referred to as "The Gabby," this involves talking too much and meandering around the topic without getting to the point. Such a tendency can overwhelm the listener with unnecessary details and obscure the main message. Additionally, it can lead to the listener losing interest or feeling that their time isn't being valued.

Oversharing: Diving too deeply into personal information or revealing sensitive details without gauging the comfort level of the audience can derail a conversation. While openness can be appreciated, excessive sharing might catch listeners off-guard, making them feel uneasy or placed in an awkward position. This can not only divert the conversation from its intended path but also potentially strain the rapport between the participants. It's essential to strike a balance and be discerning about the amount and type of information shared, especially in mixed companies or more formal settings.

Not Saying How You Feel: Suppressing or masking your genuine emotions and thoughts can create a barrier to authentic communication. While there might be instances where discretion is necessary, consistently holding back can prevent both parties from reaching a deeper level of understanding and connection. Whether in personal or professional settings, being open and honest, while still being tactful, can pave the way for more transparent and enriching interactions.

Ignoring Non-Verbal Cues: Communication extends far beyond the spoken word. Our body language, facial expressions, and tone of voice often convey messages just as powerfully, if not more so, than our words. Neglecting or misinterpreting these non-verbal signals can result in significant misunderstandings. Being attuned to these cues, both in expressing oneself and in interpreting others is crucial for a holistic understanding of any interaction. It's essential to be aware of the silent messages we send and receive to ensure clear and effective communication.

Talking at, Not With: Communication should be a two-way street. When one person dominates the conversation, it can feel as though they are talking "at" others rather than "with" them. This approach can stifle open dialogue, making others feel unheard or undervalued. It's essential to strike a balance, allowing space for everyone to share their perspectives and contribute to the conversation. By ensuring that communication is reciprocal, we foster an environment of mutual respect and understanding, where all voices are valued.

Assuming Understanding: It's easy to believe that others are on the same page as we are, especially when discussing familiar topics or within close relationships. However, presuming that others automatically grasp our meaning without verifying can be a pitfall. It's essential to occasionally pause, seek feedback, and ask clarifying questions to ensure that both parties are aligned in their understanding. By taking this extra step, we can foster clearer communication and reduce the chances of misunderstandings.

These pitfalls are common, and we all fall into them from time to time. But being aware of these potential blocks and actively working to avoid them can lead to more enjoyable interactions.

Communication is not a static skill; it's a dynamic process that can always be refined and improved. One of the most effective ways to enhance communication abilities is by seeking feedback and taking time to reflect on one's style. By asking for feedback from others, individuals can gain insight into what they're doing well and where they might need improvement. This external perspective can reveal blind spots that might not be apparent otherwise. By understanding where challenges lie, individuals can create targeted strategies to overcome those hurdles, whether it's speaking more clearly, listening more attentively, or managing body language. Openly seeking and accepting feedback is a proactive approach that demonstrates humility and a willingness to learn and grow. It can foster trust and strengthen relationships, both personally and professionally.

Charisma and Confidence:
The Winning Duo in Small Talk

Charisma and confidence stand out as essential traits for crafting captivating and memorable exchanges in the world of casual conversations. More than just buzzwords, these characteristics can be truly powerful and transform any interaction, irrespective of its context, into something memorable and meaningful.

Charisma is a magnetic quality that draws admiration and deep regard from others and those you interact with. It's a blend of warmth, presence, and a genuine interest. Beyond mere charm or appeal, it's the profound ability to resonate with people on a deeper level and make them feel valued and special. Charismatic individuals often have a knack for storytelling, infusing conversations with anecdotes and humour to make the exchange livelier and more relatable. It's reflected in the gleam of their eye, inviting smiles and their innate talent for making others feel truly acknowledged. It's as if they're speaking directly to one's essence. Many of our admired speakers, celebrities, and role models exude these charismatic qualities. It's not just their words or actions, but the way they deliver them, with authenticity and passion, that sets them apart and makes them memorable figures in our lives.

In the context of small talk, charisma can be a game-changer. It has the power to elevate a simple exchange of pleasantries and enhance the experience for everyone involved. Whether it's a quick chat with a fellow commuter on a train or a casual exchange at a community event, charisma adds richness and friendliness to the conversation. It encourages more open and honest communication, making small talk feel less superficial and more genuine.

Charisma also has the power to break down people's barriers and defence mechanisms. It helps in creating a comfortable environment where people feel at ease to share their thoughts and feelings. In such an environment, people feel secure enough to reveal their authentic selves without apprehension or fear of judgment. This often accelerates the process of building rapport and establishing genuine connections. Yet, it's important to state that true charisma must be sincere and genuine. Overdoing it or trying too hard to be charismatic can be transparent and come across as disingenuous and off-putting. Authentic charisma comes from a place of genuine interest and empathy, coupled with self-awareness and emotional intelligence.

In conclusion, charisma is an asset in the world of small talk that adds a unique flavour to conversations. By understanding what it means to be charismatic and embracing this quality, individuals can enhance their social interactions and create more fulfilling connections. Whether in personal relationships or professional networking, charisma can be the key to leaving a lasting impression.

Confidence, on the other hand, is a trait that shines brightly in social interactions. Being confident means believing in one's capabilities and the ability to communicate with certainty. It's not about being boastful or arrogant; instead, it's a reflection of self-assuredness and comfort in one's own identity. It's like wearing an invisible badge that says, "I'm here, and

I'm me."

In the context of small talk, much like charisma, confidence can be a game-changer. When someone speaks with confidence, they often radiate a positive energy that draws others in. They ask thoughtful questions, offer valuable insights, and engage actively, creating a dynamic and interactive conversation. Their confidence inspires and puts others at ease. It permits others to be themselves and encourages them to share more openly and participate more fully in the discussion.

Confidence also helps in navigating the unexpected twists and turns that can arise in casual conversation. A confident communicator can smoothly steer the conversation in a new direction or gracefully handle a potentially awkward moment. In essence, being confident in small talk revolves around authenticity, attentiveness, and presence in the moment. It involves believing in oneself and valuing the connection with others. With such confidence, even basic conversations can transform into significant experiences, building trust and enhancing relationships.

When combined, charisma and confidence become a winning duo. Charisma allows you to connect with others on a personal level, making conversations more engaging, while confidence establishes a foundation of trust and mutual admiration. These attributes seamlessly complement each other: the confidence inherent in a charismatic individual shines through in their attentive listening and thoughtful responses, and in turn, this confidence amplifies the authenticity and presence that define charisma. Cultivating charisma and confidence is about recognizing your unique worth and being willing to share that with others. It requires consistent practice, self-awareness, and a sincere desire to engage with others. By homing in on these two qualities, you can enhance your conversational abilities and enjoy more fulfilling and more rewarding social exchanges.

Building Charisma and Confidence: A Practical Guide

1. Practice Active Listening:

   - Exercise: Dedicate yourself to a conversation where your primary role is to listen actively. Maintain steady eye contact, nod in acknowledgement, and ask insightful follow-up questions to demonstrate your genuine engagement. Avoid interrupting or steering the conversation; let the other person take the lead.

   - Outcome: This practice not only sharpens your listening skills but also deepens your ability to connect with others on a meaningful level, which is a cornerstone of charisma. Over time, this exercise can help you become a more empathetic and attentive conversationalist, qualities that are highly valued in any social interaction.

2. Work on Body Language:

   - Exercise: Find a quiet space and stand in front of a mirror. Begin by practicing confident postures: stand tall with your shoulders back and chin slightly raised. Maintain steady eye contact with your reflection, allowing a genuine smile to form. Incorporate open gestures, such as palms facing upwards or hands resting comfortably at your sides, avoiding crossed arms or closed-off stances. As you do this, observe the changes in your demeanour and the energy you project.

   - Outcome: Regularly practicing these postures not only helps in making you appear more confident and approachable but also instils a genuine sense of self-assuredness. Over time, this exercise can enhance your natural charisma, making you more magnetic and relatable in social situations.

3. Develop a Personal Elevator Pitch:

   - Exercise: Take a moment to reflect on your interests, strengths, and unique qualities. Now, craft a 30-second introduction about yourself that encapsulates these elements. Practice delivering this introduction with enthusiasm and authenticity, ensuring your tone is engaging and your body language is open and confident. Rehearse this introduction multiple times until it feels natural.

   - Outcome: Regularly practicing this introduction not only builds confidence in presenting yourself but also ensures you make a charismatic and memorable first impression. Being prepared with a well-thought-out introduction can set the tone for positive and engaging interactions, whether in professional settings or casual encounters

4. Role-play Different Scenarios:

   - Exercise: Partner up with a friend and simulate various social scenarios. For each scenario, experiment with different elements of communication: adjust your tone from enthusiastic to serious, modify your body language from open to reserved, and vary the content of your conversation from light-hearted to deep. As you go through each variation, discuss with your friend the impact of these changes and gather feedback.

   - Outcome: Engaging in this exercise allows you to become more versatile in your communication style. By understanding the effects of different tones, body languages, and content, you can better tailor your approach to different social situations. This adaptability not only enhances your charisma by making you more relatable and engaging but also boosts your confidence as you become more adept at navigating diverse interactions.

5. Set Small Social Challenges:

   - Challenge yourself with incremental social tasks, starting with simple gestures like complimenting a stranger on their attire or initiating a casual conversation with a colleague about their weekend plans. As you become more comfortable, increase the complexity of your interactions, perhaps by joining group discussions or attending social events outside your usual circle.

   - Outcome: By progressively stepping out of your comfort zone and engaging in varied social interactions, you cultivate resilience and adaptability in social settings. This iterative approach not only builds confidence in your ability to handle diverse conversational scenarios but also refines your interpersonal skills, making you more adept at navigating and contributing to discussions.

7. Visualization Techniques:

   - Exercise: Take a few moments in a quiet space to visualize a successful social interaction. Imagine the setting, the people involved, and the flow of the conversation. Focus on the emotions you want to experience, such as joy, ease, or enthusiasm, and how you want to present yourself — confident, attentive, and charismatic. Picture yourself navigating the interaction with grace, responding thoughtfully, and leaving a positive impression.

   - Outcome: This mental rehearsal primes your brain for success. By consistently visualizing positive outcomes, you begin to internalize these scenarios, making it easier to manifest them in real life. This not only bolsters your confidence but also equips you with a mental blueprint for navigating social situations effectively.

8. Join a Public Speaking Group:

   - Exercise: Join a local public speaking club or group, such as Toastmasters or a similar organization. Engage actively by giving speeches, participating in impromptu speaking sessions, and seeking out roles that challenge you to communicate in front of an audience.

   - Outcome: Immersing yourself in a structured and supportive environment dedicated to honing communication skills allows you to practice conveying ideas with charisma and speaking with confidence. Regular feedback from peers and mentors in these settings helps pinpoint areas for growth, while consistent practice reinforces positive habits, ultimately enhancing your ability to engage and influence audiences both large and small.

9. Seek Feedback:

   - Exercise: Approach trusted friends or family members and request their candid feedback on your communication style, presence, and overall demeanour during conversations. Encourage them to provide specific examples and highlight both strengths and areas where you might refine your approach.

   - Outcome: Receiving feedback from those who know you well can provide invaluable insights into how you come across to others. This exercise not only helps identify areas for improvement but also reinforces positive behaviours and habits you already exhibit. By understanding others' perceptions, you can work towards enhancing your charisma and confidence in interactions.

These skills are not static but can be developed and refined over time. By incorporating these exercises into daily life, you can actively work on enhancing charisma and confidence.

Beyond Words: Exploring Body Language, Facial Expressions and Tonality in Conversation

Words are just the tip of the iceberg, a mere fraction of the intricate tapestry of human communication. Beneath the surface lies a vast and often unexplored reservoir of non-verbal cues, including body language, facial expressions, and tone of voice. These silent signals, often speak louder than words, acting as a powerful undercurrent that shapes our interactions.

Non-verbal communication is like a hidden language that we all speak without our conscious awareness. It's a universal form of expression that transcends cultural and linguistic barriers, revealing emotions and intentions that words might overlook or misconstrue. It's the spontaneous grin that surfaces when recalling a cherished moment or a funny memory. It's the instinctive folding of arms when we feel defensive, or the reassuring pat on the back when a friend is upset that says, "I'm here for you." This unspoken language is not just an accessory to conversation; it's an essential component that adds depth and dimension to our interactions. It offers a backdrop, enhances comprehension and often reveals truths that words might conceal.

In a world where we are often focused on what we say, understanding the power of what we don't say is enlightening. It invites us to be more observant and more connected to those around us. It challenges us to look beyond the words and tune in to the silent symphony of gestures, expressions, and tones that make our interactions truly human. It's about recognizing that sometimes, the most profound conversations happen in silence.

Body language, for instance, offers a window into a person's comfort level, emotions and sometimes even their true thoughts, which might differ from what's being said verbally. Take, for example, a person who insists they're fine but displays a slouched posture or crossed arms. Such physical indicators might suggest a sense of discomfort, defensiveness, or even disagreement with what's being discussed. Even when someone attempts to mask their emotions, the body frequently reveals them through these small, yet unconscious movements.

Standing tall with shoulders back is more than just good posture; it's a powerful form that can express confidence and assertiveness. This stance takes up more space and often conveys a sense of self-assurance and control. It can make a person appear more authoritative and can be particularly effective in professional or formal settings where demonstrating leadership or competence is essential.

Hand movements are also a dynamic and expressive component of our body language. They can provide context and add emphasis to our points. For instance, open palms, typically with hands facing upwards, is a widely recognized gesture indicating honesty, openness, or a willingness to engage. It's as if the person is saying, "See, I have nothing to hide," or "I'm open to your ideas."

However, it's important to recognize that body language is complex and context-dependent. Cultural differences, personal habits, or even the ambient temperature can influence these gestures. A slouched posture in a casual setting among friends might not carry the same connotations as in a business meeting. Similarly, someone might cross their arms because they're cold or trying to soothe themselves in a stressful situation, not because they're being defensive or resistant. As such, it's always beneficial to consider the broader context and combine these non-verbal cues with verbal communication to get a more accurate understanding of the situation and to respond appropriately.

Our faces are like canvases. They are incredibly expressive, often revealing more than words ever could. Every twitch of a muscle, every raise of an eyebrow, and every slight curve of the lips can unveil a spectrum of feelings. A faint smile can convey a multitude of emotions. It could signify genuine happiness, a polite response, or sometimes a mask for underlying sadness. The eyes often complement this, either shining with delight or shadowed by unspoken pain. On the other hand, a gentle frown, even if momentary, can indicate concern, deep thought, or mild confusion. It acts as a quiet call for understanding or a testament to compassion. Moreover, the nuances of facial expressions can vary based on cultural and individual differences. What's considered a warm, friendly smile in one culture might be seen as disingenuous in another. Likewise, a slight narrowing of the eyes might indicate scepticism for one individual, while for another, it could simply be a sign of intense focus.

Beyond the obvious expressions, countless micro-expressions flash across our faces in fractions of a second, often betraying our true feelings before we have a chance to hide them. These quick, involuntary facial movements can provide keen observers with a window into true emotions. In conversations, recognizing and responding to these facial cues can greatly enhance understanding and connection. By tuning into these subtle expressions, we can gain deeper insights into the emotions and thoughts of our conversational partners.

Eye contact is one of the most powerful tools in non-verbal communication. When we maintain eye contact during a conversation, it sends a clear message of engagement, attentiveness, and genuine interest in the person we're speaking with. It shows the other person that we value the interaction and are actively listening to what they have to say. This simple act can foster trust, create a sense of intimacy, and build rapport between individuals regardless of the context. On the flip side, consistently avoiding eye contact can convey a different message. It might indicate discomfort, perhaps stemming from nervousness or unease in the situation. Some people might divert their gaze because they're processing information or are lost in thought. In certain contexts, avoiding eye contact might be perceived as a sign of dishonesty or evasiveness, as if one is trying to hide something.

Interestingly, cultural norms also play a significant role in how eye contact is interpreted. In certain cultures, such as in parts of Asia and Africa, extended eye contact can be perceived as aggressive or disrespectful, indicating a challenge or intrusion into personal space. Conversely, in many Western cultures, like those in the United States and Western Europe, sustained eye contact is often viewed as a mark of sincerity and confidence, conveying attentiveness and interest in the conversation. Furthermore, for individuals with specific neurodivergent conditions, maintaining prolonged eye contact can be difficult. In such cases, it's crucial to approach the situation with compassion and sensitivity.

Too much eye contact can feel intense and overwhelming. It might come across as staring, which can be perceived as aggressive, confrontational, or simply rude. When someone maintains unbroken eye contact for extended periods, it can make the other person feel scrutinized or under pressure, as if they're being challenged or evaluated. This can create a barrier in the conversation. On the other hand, too little eye contact can be equally problematic. If someone consistently avoids meeting another's gaze, it can lead to feelings of disconnect and might make the other person question the sincerity of the interaction.

Striking the right balance is essential. Being fully present and sensitive to the other person's comfort can make all the difference. Observing their reactions and adjusting our eye contact in response can lead to deeper and more comfortable exchanges. While eye contact can reveal a spectrum of feelings and intentions, it's vital to view it within the larger context and recognize individual differences when interpreting its meaning.

Tonality can be compared to the spectrum of colours in a painting. Just as different shades can elicit diverse feelings in artwork, the subtle variations in our voice add richness and sentiment to our words. It's not just what we say, but how we say it that truly matters.

Consider the phrase, "Are you coming?" When spoken with an upward inflection, it's a genuine question, seeking clarity. But with a flat tone, it might convey impatience or even annoyance. The same words, but with entirely different implications based on tonality alone. Similarly, the phrase "That's an interesting idea" perfectly illustrates how tone can change a message's meaning. Delivered with enthusiasm, it feels like genuine praise, making the listener feel their idea is valued. However, with a hint of sarcasm, it can sound like veiled criticism, potentially making the listener second-guess their contribution. If said neutrally, it's merely an acknowledgement without conveying any strong feelings. The same words can encourage, criticize, or simply acknowledge, all based on the speaker's tone. This highlights the importance of not just what we say, but how we say it. The nuances in our voice can either enhance understanding or lead to potential misunderstandings.

The volume of our voice also plays a significant role. Whispering can create intimacy, making the listener lean in and feel like they're being let in on a secret. On the other hand, speaking loudly can command attention, but if overused or misapplied, it can also come off as domineering or aggressive.

Pitch, too, has its part to play. A higher pitch can convey excitement or surprise, while a lower pitch might be interpreted as seriousness or even authority. Being attuned to these vocal nuances and adapting them based on the situation and the listener can make conversations more effective. By being mindful of our tonality, we can ensure our words are not just heard, but truly understood.

Our movements and gait, often overlooked, are clues to our internal state and can reveal a lot about our emotions and personality. Take the way we walk, for example. A brisk, purposeful stride often suggests confidence, energy, and a clear sense of direction. It might be the walk of someone who knows exactly where they're going, both literally and metaphorically. On the other hand, a slow, hesitant walk, especially with slouched shoulders, can be indicative of fatigue, melancholy, or introspection. Such a pace could represent an individual weighed down by worries, deep in thought, or simply having a low-energy day.

Moreover, someone with a bouncy, springy step often radiates positivity and liveliness, while deliberate, even-paced steps can suggest a more cautious and thoughtful personality. This is akin to the way someone navigates a room – whether they move fluidly, avoiding obstacles with grace, or move hesitantly – can also give insights into their confidence levels and familiarity with the environment.

In essence, our movements, often subconscious, are a continuous dance of communication. Understanding these different types of body language can enhance our ability to read others and convey our messages more adeptly. It's a fascinating aspect of human interaction that goes beyond words.

The Unspoken Art: Tips for Perfecting the Craft of Non-Verbal Communication

1. Facial Expression Exercise: A great way to understand facial expressions is to practice them. Using a mirror, practice conveying various emotions such as happiness, sadness, surprise, anger, etc using only your facial expressions. Noticing subtle details, such

as a raised eyebrow or the slight curl of the lips, helps in enhancing one's expressiveness and identifying these emotions and signals in others.

2. Honing Observational Skills: Head to a public place like a local park, café, or any lively area and discreetly observe people. Try to guess their emotions or the nature of their conversations based on their body language. This exercise sharpens your observational skills and helps you decode non-verbal cues more effectively.

3. The Silent Conversation: Pair up with a friend for this one. Sit facing each other and engage in a conversation using only gestures, facial expressions, and body language. It might feel a bit silly at first, but it's a fantastic way that underscore the power and nuances of non-verbal communication.

4. Exploring Tonality: Read a neutral sentence, like "The cat sat on the mat," in various emotional tones. This helps in understanding how the same words can convey different meanings based solely on tonality and how tonality can change the perceived meaning of words.

5. Mindful Posture: Throughout the day, be mindful of your posture. Are you slouching at your desk? Standing lopsided while waiting for the bus? Every hour, do a quick posture check. Over time, maintaining a balanced and open posture becomes second nature, conveying confidence and openness to those around you.

6. Understanding Touch: With a willing participant, practice different types of touch – a pat on the back, a handshake, a touch on the arm and discuss how each feels and the emotions they convey. This exercise fosters an understanding of touch's role in communication.

7. Walking Dynamics: Pay attention to your walk. Is it brisk and purposeful? Slow and contemplative? Try altering your walk and notice how it affects your mood and how others perceive you. A confident stride can often set the tone for an interaction.

Breaking the Ice:

Crafting Perfect Conversation Starters

In conversation, the saying "knowledge is power" rings true. Understanding your audience is paramount when initiating dialogue. Whether it's a post-meeting discussion with a co-worker, a conversation with someone you're interested in romantically, or a first-time introduction at a social gathering, adjusting your approach based on the individual can make all the difference. For instance, with a colleague, you might kick off the conversation by discussing a work-related development or an upcoming project. With a potential romantic interest, perhaps a light-hearted compliment or discussing a mutual hobby could be a good starting point. Meanwhile, at a social event, commenting on the occasion or discussing someone you both know might be a safe bet.

Being attuned to the context and the person not only helps in crafting a relevant conversation starter but also demonstrates attentiveness and respect. It shows that you're not just following a script but genuinely interested in building a connection. By taking a moment to consider who you're speaking to, you set the stage for a more meaningful and engaging conversation.

Relevance is Key: The Significance of Finding Common Ground in Dialogue

Finding a common thread to initiate a conversation can sometimes feel like charting unknown waters, especially when interacting with individuals from varied backgrounds or in unfamiliar environments. The quest for that perfect starting point, a topic that resonates with both parties, requires a delicate balance of observation, intuition, and courage. Luckily for us, there are some topics that serve as universal connectors. This is where the concept of relevance comes into play. By focusing on topics that are universally relatable and easily understood, we can ease past the initial awkwardness and lay the foundation for meaningful dialogue. Certainly, topics like current events, weather, food, travel, and work or study stand out as effective conversation starters. Let's delve into why these topics are so impactful.

Current Events: The world around us is in a constant state of flux. Be it global news or local happenings, events are continuously unfolding influencing societies, cultures, and individual lives. Discussing current events offers an immediate touchpoint, as these topics are fresh and at the forefront of people's minds. This could range from the outcome of a recent sports game, or a significant political event, to the latest technological breakthrough. Current events provide a shared reality for people to share opinions, express concerns, or simply exchange information. Nevertheless, it's important to approach potentially divisive topics with sensitivity to ensure the conversation remains respectful and open-minded.

Weather: Often dismissed as a cliché, the weather remains one of the most universally relatable topics. Regardless of background or personal interests, everyone experiences and has an opinion on the weather. It's an immediate shared experience, whether it's expressing disappointment over unexpected rain or marvelling at a particularly beautiful sunset. Initiating a conversation with a remark about the weather can also naturally segue into other topics, from plans affected by the weather memories triggered by certain weather conditions.

Work or Study: While it's a topic best approached with some tact (to avoid any sensitive areas), discussing one's profession or academic pursuits can be insightful. It sheds light on how someone spends a significant portion of their time and what they're passionate about. Whether it's a recent project, challenges faced, or aspirations for the future, discussing work or study can provide a deeper understanding of a person's ambitions, hurdles, and daily life.

Travel: Whether it's a weekend getaway or a trip across continents, travel is a topic everyone is excited to talk about. It's often infused with a mix of enthusiasm and curiosity, given the myriad of experiences, lessons, and dreams it encompasses. Even those who haven't recently travelled, often have places on their wish list they dream of visiting. Sharing travel stories has the power to take both the speaker and the listener on a journey to various destinations, introducing them to diverse cultures, landscapes, and experiences. Furthermore, delving into travel discussions can uncover mutual interests, past adventures, or upcoming itineraries.

Food: A universal love that is another delightful conversation starter. Food is more than just sustenance; it's a reflection of culture, tradition, and personal preference. Everyone eats, and most people have strong feelings or memories associated with certain dishes or cuisines. Asking someone about their favourite restaurant in town, exchanging recipes, or even their go-to comfort food can open the door to rich stories and shared recommendations. Food, with its sensory and emotional connections, offers a delicious avenue to explore shared experiences and tastes.

These conversation starters, rooted in shared experiences and interests, can be tailored to suit the context and the people involved. By homing in on topics that resonate with everyone, we can overcome the initial hurdles of unfamiliarity, paving the way for interactions grounded in mutual understanding and interest.

Spotting the Immediate: The Art of Observational Conversation Starters

Simply enough, sometimes the most effective way to weave a connection during conversation is by commenting on the immediate and observable. It's a strategy as old as conversation itself, and for a good reason: it works.

Picture walking into a room with a striking piece of artwork taking centre stage or attending an event with a particularly lively atmosphere. These immediate surroundings offer a wealth of topics that can be delved into. Commenting on the ambience of a place, the music playing in the background, or even the delightful (or unusual) taste of the appetizers at an event can be the perfect icebreaker. Why does this approach resonate so well? Firstly, it's neutral ground. Unlike diving into personal topics or potentially divisive subjects, the immediate environment is a shared experience. Both you and the person you're speaking to are in the same setting, experiencing the same sights, sounds, and sensations. This mutual experience provides an immediate commonality.

Furthermore, discussing something observable can lead to a cascade of other relatable topics. For instance, a simple comment about a beautiful chandelier can lead to a discussion about interior design, personal aesthetic preferences, or even memorable places someone visited. Similarly, pointing out a catchy song playing in the background can spiral into discussions about musical tastes, favourite music genres, concerts attended in the past, musical talents or even the nostalgic memories tied to certain melodies. Such organic flow in conversation not only keeps the dialogue engaging but also allows participants to discover shared interests and experiences.

Finally, shifting the focus to the immediate environment offers an inclusive way to engage. It eliminates the need for prior knowledge or shared history, therefore, regardless of who you're conversing with, everyone can contribute to the conversation.

In the end, using the immediate and observable as a conversation starter is like picking up a book and reading the first page together. It's a collective experience of discovery, one that can lead to deeper discussions, mutual understanding and impactful interactions.

The Genuine Compliment: A Sincere Start to Meaningful Conversations

Compliments, our ego loves them. They carry a unique charm, striking a chord within us and making us feel seen and appreciated. When wielded with sincerity and genuine appreciation, they become more than just words. They transform into powerful tools that can foster trust, break barriers, and open doors. These simple melding of words have the power to not only initiate conversations but also to set a positive tone for the interaction that follows.

Everyone appreciates a moment of recognition. Whether it's for their attributes, their sense of style, their accomplishments, or even their choice of book they're reading at a café. When you notice and acknowledge these details, it sends a clear message: "I see you, and I appreciate what I see." This simple acknowledgement can boost our mood, validate our efforts, and create a sense of belonging. This can be the spark that ignites a conversation. However, the key to this strategy lies in the word "genuine." Compliments, to truly resonate, must come from a place of honesty. People have an innate ability to discern between a sincere compliment and one that's given out of obligation or with an ulterior motive. An insincere compliment not only misses the mark but can turn people off, making the subsequent conversation feel forced, awkward or inauthentic.

So, how does one ensure their compliments are genuine you say? Well, the key lies in being fully present in the moment and not just going through the motions. It's about observing with an open heart, free from preconceived notions or biases and expressing what genuinely stands out to you. It's less about flattery or saying something for the sake of it and more about recognizing and appreciating the qualities or efforts of the person in front of you. By approaching compliments with this mindset, it can be the first steps towards a blossoming relationship or a strengthened bond.

So, if you see something you like or something about a person catches your eye, voice it. Tell them and share your appreciation. Compliments are a powerful tool to have in the conversational toolkit and by ensuring they stem from a genuine place, you set the stage for conversations that are both engaging and sincere.

Humour in Conversation: Striking the Balance

Everyone, no matter where they are from or what their background is, enjoys a good laugh. It's a universal language that transcends boundaries and cultures. It releases endorphins, our body's feel-good chemicals and makes us feel uplifted and connected.

Humour, with its infectious energy, has long been a favoured tool in the conversational arsenal. When used effectively, it can break the ice and lighten the mood. When people laugh together, barriers dissolve, and distances shrink. It's a communal experience that fosters a sense of camaraderie and mutual understanding. Such moments of joy can bridge gaps, be they cultural, generational, or ideological. It creates a shared experience, that communicates "We see the world through a similar lens." However, like any tool, its impact hinges on its application.

Using humour as an icebreaker serves multiple purposes. To begin with, it showcases vulnerability. By making a joke or sharing a funny story, you reveal a glimpse of your personality, inviting others to do the same.

Additionally, humour acts as a window into an individual's character. Through their comedic expression, it provides insights into their perspective, creative flair, and even core beliefs. This peek into their character can make them more relatable and endearing to others. Along with that, humour has been shown to have significant physiological and psychological impacts that make it a potent tool for connection. From diminishing stress hormone levels and serving as a form of cardiovascular workout, elevating heart rates and boosting blood circulation, to its ability to defuse tension in high-strung or potentially contentious situations. A well-timed joke can create a more collaborative and relaxed atmosphere.

Yet, the line between a joke that lands and one that flops—or worse, offends—is thin. This is where the risk of humour comes into play. Humour is subjective; what one person finds hilarious, another might find confusing or even inappropriate. Factors like cultural nuances, personal experiences, and individual preferences play a key role in how humour is received.

The key to navigating this delicate balance is twofold: reading the room and knowing your audience. "Reading the room" involves being attuned to the environment and the mood of the people around you. It's about sensing the collective vibe and determining whether humour is appropriate or a fitting addition. On the other hand, "knowing your audience" emphasizes the importance of understanding the backgrounds, preferences, and potential sensitivities of those you're conversing with. A joke that might be a hit at a comedy club could be a misstep in a more formal setting or with a diverse group.

In conclusion, the goal is to unite, not alienate. While humour is a powerful conversation starter and can be a game-changer in social situations, its success is deeply connected to the context in which it is used. By being observant, empathetic, and considerate, one can effectively utilize humour, making sure that the laughter it evokes is shared by all. This approach might just be the secret to turning acquaintances into friends.

From Observation to Interaction: Inviting Engagement in Conversation

There's a subtle art to turning a monologue into a dialogue. While posing questions is the most direct way route to engage someone, making statements that invite a response can be just as effective, if not more so. This method turns a simple observation into a springboard for two-way interaction, creating an environment where both parties feel involved and included.

Imagine you're at a botanical garden. Instead of asking, "Do you like these flowers?", you might comment, "The fragrance of these flowers is so refreshing. It reminds me of my grandmother's garden back home." Such a statement does more than just convey an observation; it extends an implicit invitation for the other person to share their perspective, feelings, or a related memory. They might reply with their favourite flower in the garden or share a story about a special place they once visited related to the topic. The beauty of this approach lies in its organic nature. It doesn't put the other person on the spot with a direct question but rather offers them an open door to walk through if they choose. It's a gentle nudge that says, "Here's what I think; I'd love to hear your thoughts too." Furthermore, this approach highlights a proactive engagement with the surroundings and the subject being discussed. It demonstrates that you're not just passively observing but actively reflecting and connecting, which can inspire the other person to do the same.

Incorporating this technique into conversations can be surprisingly straightforward. Whether commenting on the decor in a café, the aroma of a dish, or the plot twist in a movie, the goal is to share in a way that leaves room for expansion. It's like setting the stage and then stepping back, allowing the other person to play a starring role in the unfolding conversation.

It's a reminder that the most memorable interactions aren't just about speaking but also about creating spaces for listening and mutual exchange.

The Role of Practice and Feedback

The path to perfecting this craft is much like chiselling a statue from stone. It requires patience, practice, and a touch of finesse. Just as each stone has its distinct texture and grain, every conversation and its participants bring their own uniqueness. It's about finding that sweet spot where preparation meets spontaneity. Hence, it's essential to refine your approach based on feedback and personal experience, ensuring your conversation starters feel both natural and effective. Here's how to go about it:

Diverse Practice Grounds: Begin by venturing out of your comfort zone. Try initiating conversations in various settings, be it at a local coffee shop, during a community event, or even in an online forum. Each environment offers a different dynamic, which makes it a good practice ground to adapt and refine your approach.

Welcome Feedback: It's natural to shy away or get defensive when it comes to receiving feedback, especially when it's not all praise. However, such insights are invaluable. If you're conversing with a trusted friend or colleague, seek their perspective post-conversation. Did your opener feel genuine? Was there a point where the conversation felt forced? Their observations can provide tangible areas for improvement.

Introspection: After a conversation, especially one that felt particularly challenging or rewarding, take a moment to reflect. What went well? What could you have done differently? How did you feel overall? Self-assessment is a powerful tool for understanding your strengths and areas for growth in addition to the external feedback you receive.

Adjust and Adapt: Not every conversation starter will be a hit, and that's okay. The key is to recognize when something doesn't work and adjust accordingly. Maybe a particular question felt too intrusive, or perhaps a joke didn't land as expected. Use these moments as learning opportunities.

Stay Authentic: While refining your approach is important, it's equally important to stay true to yourself. Conversations should feel genuine, not like a rehearsed performance. Over time, as you gather more experience and feedback, you'll find a style that's both effective and authentically you.

Navigating Group Conversations: Strategies for Engaging Multiple People

Understanding group dynamics is crucial for anyone aspiring to excel in small talk. There are various moments in our lives where we often find ourselves needing to engage with and even entertain multiple individuals simultaneously and to the average person, this is a daunting task. Conversing within a group brings its unique set of challenges and opportunities. Unlike direct one-on-one conversations, where the dynamics are relatively straightforward, group settings introduce multiple personalities, viewpoints, and conversational styles into the mix.

Group dynamics refer to the patterns of interaction between individuals in a group. These patterns can be influenced by numerous factors, such as the relationships between group members, individual personalities, the topic of discussion, and even the environment where the conversation takes place. Recognizing and adapting to these dynamics can significantly impact the flow and outcome of a conversation. For instance, in a group where several members already know each other well, there might be established patterns of communication, inside jokes, or shared experiences that a newcomer might not be privy to. In such scenarios, the newcomer might feel awkward, left out or find it challenging to contribute meaningfully to the conversation. Conversely, groups with members from varied backgrounds and experiences can bring a wealth of diverse viewpoints to a discussion. However, such diversity might also require more effort in terms of establishing common ground and ensuring that everyone feels acknowledged and included.

Power dynamics can also come into play. In professional settings, for example, the presence of a senior executive might subtly or overtly influence the contributions of others. Some might tread more cautiously, choosing their words with extra care or even holding back certain viewpoints. This restraint might come from a desire to avoid upsetting or potentially challenging someone with a higher authority. Being attuned to these dynamics allows participants to adjust their communication strategies.

Confidence and Assertiveness in Group Conversations

Within group discussions, it's not uncommon for voices to get drowned out or for some individuals to take a backseat, letting the more dominant personalities lead the conversation. However, the importance of hearing from every participant cannot be overstated, as each brings a distinct viewpoint to the table. This is where the virtues of confidence and assertiveness come to the forefront.

As discussed in the previous chapter *Charisma and Confidence: The Winning duo in Small Talk*, confidence is the belief in one's abilities and the value of one's contributions. It's the internal compass that reminds us that our opinions and insights are valid and worthy of being shared. On the other hand, assertiveness is the ability to express oneself and one's views in a straightforward and respectful manner. It's about standing your ground, not aggressively, but with poise and clarity. In group settings, these qualities ensure that an individual doesn't just become background furniture. Instead, they participate actively, contribute meaningfully, and help steer the direction of conversation. This isn't about overshadowing others or monopolizing the dialogue. It's about waiting for the right moment, speaking clearly, and ensuring that your points are articulated well.

Being confident and assertive has broader implications beyond the immediate conversation. It sets a precedent for future interactions, indicating to others that you are someone who values their own voice and expects the same respect in return. Over time, this can elevate your standing and sway within a group or community. However, it's essential to strike a balance. While asserting your presence is key, it's equally important to be an attentive listener and remain open to the perspectives of others. After all, true communication is as much about listening as it is about speaking.

While the ins and outs of group conversations can be challenging to navigate, confidence and assertiveness are invaluable tools in ensuring that one's voice is heard. By believing in the worth of our contributions and having the courage to share them, we not only elevate the discussion but also pave the way for more inclusive and balanced interactions.

Ensuring Equitable Participation: Handling Dominant Speakers

Group conversations can be unique and exhilarating. Different from one-on-one interactions, they present a melting pot of diverse thoughts and perspectives. Yet, occasionally, there are moments when the harmony of these interactions can become sour, particularly when a select few take centre stage and dominate the conversation. While these dominant speakers might have valuable things to say, promoting participation from all enriches the conversation and creates a space of respect and inclusivity. Here are some tactics to manage dominant speakers and create a more balanced dialogue:

1. Set Clear Ground Rules: At the beginning of a discussion, especially in formal settings like meetings, it's beneficial to establish ground rules. This might include guidelines like allowing one person to speak at a time or setting time limits for individual contributions.

2. Active Moderation: If you're leading the conversation, take an active role in moderating or if your group meets regularly, rotate the role of the facilitator. This can change the group's dynamics and allow different members to set the tone and pace of discussions. In more structured settings, creating a speaking order or having a predetermined speaking order can ensure everyone gets a turn. This can be especially useful in virtual meetings where visual cues might be harder to interpret.

3. Inviting Participation: If you notice someone hasn't spoken for a while, gently interrupt dominant speakers when necessary and invite quieter participants to share their thoughts. Phrases like "Let's hear from someone we haven't heard from yet" can be effective. Additionally, if one person is dominating, acknowledge their contribution and then redirect. For instance, "Thank you for that insight, Alex. I'm curious to hear what Jamie thinks about this topic."

4. Use Non-verbal Cues: Sometimes, a simple gesture can speak volumes. Raising a hand, establishing eye contact, or leaning in can indicate that another person wishes to contribute to the conversation.

5. Open-ended Questions: If certain individuals haven't had a chance to speak, direct open-ended questions their way. This can provide them with a comfortable opportunity to jump into the discussion.

6. Break into Smaller Groups: In larger gatherings, breaking into smaller discussion groups can give quieter members a more comfortable setting to share their thoughts. Afterwards, each group can relay the essence of their discussions back to the broader group.

7. Private Feedback: If you notice a specific individual always taking the lead in discussions, it might be beneficial to talk to them privately. Approach the situation with understanding, highlighting that while their enthusiasm is appreciated, it's essential for all voices to be heard. Encourage them to listen more and allow space for others to chime in.

8. Use Technology: In online environments, tools like the "raise hand" feature or the chat box can help manage the flow of conversation and ensure that everyone gets a chance to contribute.

Engaging with Multiple Personalities in Group Conversations

In any group setting, it's almost a given that you'll encounter a mix of personalities. As everyone brings a unique flavour to the conversation, understanding how to navigate and connect with varied personalities can lead to more cohesive and fruitful group interactions. Here's how you can tailor your conversation style to resonate with different personalities within a group:

The Quiet Thinker: Every group has its silent participants. They might not speak often, but when they do, their insights can be profound. Introverted or shy individuals might hold back in group settings, but that doesn't mean they have nothing to contribute. Often, they offer thoughtful insights when given the opportunity. Create space for them by asking open-ended questions or seeking their opinion directly: "Lena, you've worked on a similar project. Do you have any insights to share?" This shows them that their voice is valued.

The Detail-Oriented Person: Some individuals thrive on specifics and details. They can provide depth to a conversation, ensuring that important nuances aren't overlooked. However, if the discussion becomes too granular, it might be helpful to steer it back to the broader topic: "Those details are crucial, Trey. Let's also consider the bigger picture. How does this fit into our overall goal?"

The Big-Picture Visionary: Opposite to the detail-oriented individual, the visionary often speaks in broad strokes, focusing on overarching themes and ideas. While their contributions can be inspiring, it's sometimes necessary to ground the discussion in practical terms. "I love that vision, Priya. How can we start implementing that in the next quarter?"

The Devil's Advocate: This individual often presents opposing viewpoints, not necessarily because they disagree, but to ensure all angles are considered. While this can be invaluable for thorough decision-making, it's essential to ensure that the conversation remains constructive. "It's good to consider all sides, Alicia. Let's also discuss potential solutions."

The Sceptic: Cautious and often questioning, sceptics need convincing. They tend to challenge assertions and ask for evidence. Engaging with them requires patience and a willingness to justify your points. Their scepticism, while sometimes demanding, can lead to more thorough and well-rounded discussions.

The Consensus Builder: Often diplomatic, this person seeks common ground and tries to bring the group together. They can be instrumental in resolving disagreements. Recognize their efforts and support their role in fostering unity: "I appreciate how you're bringing different viewpoints together, Ravi. Let's build on that."

When engaging with diverse personalities, active listening is key. By truly hearing what each person has to say, you can tailor your responses to resonate with them. Fostering an environment of respect and openness encourages all participants, regardless of their personality type, to contribute meaningfully. Remember, the strength of a group lies in its diversity. By valuing and engaging with each unique personality, you uplift the conversation and drive collective progress.

Seamless Transitions: Keeping Group Conversations Flowing

During the ebbs and flows of group conversation, ensuring a smooth transition between topics is akin to a conductor guiding an orchestra through different movements of a symphony. It's about maintaining rhythm, interest, and engagement. Perfecting this skill can make discussions more fruitful and prevent them from becoming stagnant or veering off track.

One of the simplest ways to transition is by posing an open-ended question related to the current topic. This allows participants to share their perspectives and naturally introduces new subtopics. For instance, after discussing a recent film, you might ask, "Speaking of movies, has anyone seen any good series lately?" Sharing a brief personal story also can bridge the gap between two topics. If the group is discussing travel destinations and you wish to shift to food, you might mention a memorable meal you had while travelling.

Bringing up recent news or events can be a great way to introduce a new topic. For example, if the conversation is about technology, mentioning a recent tech-related headline can shift the discussion to the implications of that news. The classic "Speaking of" technique is another transition tool. If someone mentions they've been reading a lot during their commute to work, you can segue with, "Speaking of reading, have you guys heard about the new book by...?" If a topic is reaching its natural conclusion or isn't resonating with the group very well, acknowledge what's been said and introduce a new subject. "That's an interesting point about urban gardening. It reminds me of the community garden initiative downtown. Has anyone visited it recently?" In situations where visual aids are available, such as during a presentation or casual gathering with photos, leverage them to facilitate transitions. Referring to a slide or an image can act as a prompt to introduce a fresh topic. And if the conversation hits a lull, circle back to an earlier point that wasn't fully explored. "Going back to what Sara mentioned earlier, I'd love to delve deeper into..."

Remember, the goal of transitioning in group conversations is to maintain engagement and ensure everyone feels included. While it's important to guide the discussion, it's equally important to be receptive, allowing the conversation to evolve organically. With practice, transitioning between topics can become a natural and effortless part of your conversational toolkit.

Navigating Sensitive Topics in Group Dynamics

Challenging, controversial, or delicate subjects will inevitably surface during group discussions, given the blend of diverse personalities, opinions, and belief systems. Such topics can elicit intense reactions and emotions, making them tricky to address. Yet, with the right approach, these issues can be broached constructively, minimising undue tension.

Firstly, it's essential to approach these topics with an open mind. Everyone comes from different backgrounds and experiences, and what might be a non-issue for one person could be deeply personal for another. Listening actively and without judgment is key, allowing for a more inclusive environment where everyone feels heard.

When a topic arises that needs to be discussed at that moment, consider establishing some ground rules. Laying down ground rules at the outset of a potentially contentious discussion can be a game-changer. This could involve ensuring everyone gets their turn to speak, steering clear of personal attacks, or setting a time limit for the discussion. If emotions run high, taking a short break can help everyone cool off and regroup. However, not every controversial topic requires an in-depth discussion right then and there, especially if the environment isn't appropriate. If a conversation is veering into uncomfortable territory, it's perfectly fine to steer it in a different direction. A simple segue like, "That's an interesting perspective, did anyone catch the latest episode of [popular TV show]?" can redirect the conversation without dismissing anyone's viewpoint. The goal is to shift the group's focus to a more relaxed and inclusive topic. If you find the need to change the topic, choose something neutral and broadly engaging. This could be a recent film, a shared experience, or even a light-hearted anecdote.

Keeping your cool and maintaining composure, especially during heated disagreements is also paramount. As emotions intensify during spirited debates, it's important to avoid raising your voice, using confrontational language, or making personal jabs. Such actions can exacerbate the situation and undermine the goal of constructive dialogue.

Acknowledging others' sentiments is vital, even if you don't align with their views. A mere acknowledgement like "I see where you're coming from" or "I hear your point" can significantly bolster rapport and make exchanges less confrontational and more personal.

More than often, beneath disagreements, there's a common ground waiting to be discovered. Concentrating on mutual values or concerns can transform a confrontational exchange into a collaborative one. Also, always be mindful of the setting. Some subjects might be better suited for private discussions rather than larger group forums. Gauge the environment and decide if it's the right place and time for the conversation.

Lastly, it's always beneficial to reflect on these discussions afterwards. Assess the conversation's highs and lows. What went well? What could have been handled better? By understanding and learning from these interactions, future conversations can be more productive and less fraught with tension. By approaching sensitive topics with care and consideration, group conversations can be an opportunity for growth. In the end, the goal is to foster understanding and connection, even when faced with challenging topics.

Navigating Complexities: Dealing with Difficult People

Sometimes, whether fortunately or unfortunately, we cross paths with individuals who, for various reasons, disrupt the flow of a smooth conversation. These "difficult" personalities can sometimes turn what should be a simple chat into a tangled web of emotions and misunderstandings. But what exactly makes a person difficult in conversations? And what are the common types of challenging personalities we might come across?

At the heart of many difficult interactions is a divergence in communication styles, expectations, or personal histories. Often, the root of the difficulty isn't necessarily the topic at hand, but rather the underlying emotions, past experiences, current stresses or even cultural differences that influence the conversation. Recognizing these underlying factors can provide a clearer understanding of the dynamics at play and offer a pathway to more effective communication.

Common Difficult Personalities:

The Dominator: This individual tends to monopolize conversations, often speaking over others and steering the topic to their interests or opinions. Their need to dominate can stem from a desire for control, a lack of awareness, or even insecurity.

The Negative Nancy: Perpetually pessimistic, this personality type often sees the glass as half empty and can bring down the mood of a conversation with their constant focus on the negative. Conversations with them might revolve around complaints, worries, or criticisms, making interactions feel low and draining.

The Evasive One: Whether it's dodging responsibility, sidestepping questions or changing the subject, especially if the topic is uncomfortable or confrontational, this individual can be frustrating to converse with as they skirt around issues.

The One-Upper: No matter what story or experience you share, this person has had one that's bigger, better, or more dramatic. Their constant need to "one-up" can stem from a desire for validation or a competitive nature.

The Aggressor: Quick to anger or take offence, the aggressor can turn even the most benign conversations into heated arguments. Their aggressive nature might be a defence mechanism or a result of past experiences.

The Know-It-All: Convinced they have all the answers, this person is quick to offer unsolicited advice or correct others, often coming off as condescending.

The Contrarian: Always playing the devil's advocate, this person seems to enjoy taking an opposing view, often just for the sake of argument.

The Silent Type: On the opposite end of the spectrum, this person offers minimal responses and engagement, making it challenging to keep the conversation flowing.

While there are numerous archetypes out there, understanding the ones mentioned isn't about labelling or pigeonholing people. Instead, it's about recognizing patterns that can inform our approach. By identifying these tendencies, we can tailor our communication strategies to ensure that conversations remain productive and respectful.

In the end, remember that every individual, including the so-called "difficult" ones, brings a unique perspective to the table. When we approach interactions with genuine empathy, we create a space of non-judgment and understanding, allowing us to see beyond surface behaviours to the underlying causes. By showing empathy, we acknowledge their feelings and perspectives, often diffusing potential conflicts. This understanding doesn't mean we have to agree with or condone challenging behaviours. Instead, it provides a foundation for more effective communication, fostering a connection even in the face of disagreement.

Setting Boundaries: The Key to Navigating Conversations with Difficult People

Boundaries act as invisible guidelines that define how we want to be treated and what we consider acceptable behaviour. They reflect our values, priorities, and self-worth. When interacting with difficult individuals, establishing and maintaining these boundaries becomes even more crucial. In such interactions, clear boundaries guide the conversation in a direction that aligns with our values. By setting and upholding these limits, we communicate our standards and ensure that even in the face of adversity, our self-respect remains intact. Let's delve into the significance of setting boundaries and how it can transform challenging conversations:

Protection of Mental and Emotional Well-being: Constant exposure to negative, aggressive, or toxic behaviour can be very draining. By setting boundaries, you protect your mental and emotional health, ensuring that you don't feel overwhelmed, stressed or disrespected.

Promotion of Constructive Dialogue: By setting boundaries, you can guide discussions away from trouble spots. By making it clear what topics or behaviours are off-limits, you can keep the discussion productive and avoid entering problematic areas.

Empowerment and Self-respect: Establishing boundaries is a way of asserting your worth. It sends a clear message that while you are open to dialogue, you also have limits that need to be respected.

Prevention of Future Conflicts: By setting boundaries early on, you can prevent potential misunderstandings or conflicts in the future. It creates a framework for how future interactions should proceed.

Clarity and Understanding: Communicated boundaries help the other person understand where you're coming from. It eliminates guesswork and sets clear expectations for the conversation.

Maintaining Control: Difficult people often try to dominate conversations or steer them in a direction that suits them. Boundaries help you maintain control over the interaction, ensuring that it remains balanced and mutual.

Facilitating Mutual Respect: While it might seem counterintuitive, setting boundaries can foster respect. When both parties understand and respect each other's limits, it paves the way for more genuine and understanding interactions.

To effectively set boundaries:

- Be Clear and Direct! First, get clear with yourself about what you're comfortable with and what you're not. Be honest. Once you're sure, communicate it and avoid being ambiguous.

- Stay Calm! Even if the other person reacts negatively, remain composed. Remember, it's your right to set boundaries.

- Reinforce When Necessary! If someone continues to overstep, gently but firmly remind them of the boundaries you've set.

- Know When to Exit! If someone persistently disregards your boundaries, it's okay to walk away, end the conversation or even distance yourself from that person.

At its core, setting boundaries isn't about isolating oneself or shutting people out. Instead, it's a proactive measure to safeguard one's well-being and emotional health. By establishing these limits, we create an environment where meaningful and respectful communication can occur, all the while ensuring that our personal space and feelings are honoured.

Managing Emotions in the Face of Difficulty

Establishing boundaries is a forward-thinking strategy, laying the groundwork for healthy interactions. On the other hand, managing our emotions comes into play when we're in the heat of the moment, helping us to thoughtfully respond rather than impulsively react. This combination of proactive and reactive measures ensures that we approach situations with clarity and handle unexpected challenges with composure.

1. Self-awareness: Take a moment to tune into your emotions and label them. By pinpointing and expressing what you're experiencing, you gain a clearer perspective, allowing you to address and navigate your feelings with greater precision and understanding.

2. Pause Before Responding: If a comment or behaviour triggers a strong emotional reaction, take a moment to pause, breathe deeply and collect your thoughts before responding. This momentary break allows you to approach the situation with clarity

and composure, ensuring that your response is measured and constructive rather than impulsive.

3. Seek Clarity: If unsure or uneasy about a comment or action, it's always beneficial to ask for clarification rather than making assumptions. This can lead to unnecessary emotional turmoil. By taking a moment to understand the intent behind the words or actions, you can prevent misunderstandings and foster a more open and constructive dialogue.

4. Limit Exposure: If a particular individual consistently triggers negative emotions, it might be time to consider reducing the frequency or duration of your interactions with that individual. This doesn't necessarily mean cutting ties completely, but rather finding a balance that protects your well-being and choosing the level of engagement that feels right for you. If completely avoiding the person isn't feasible, especially in professional settings, consider seeking mediation or a neutral third party to facilitate more constructive interactions.

While difficult conversations are an inevitable part of life, they don't have to be destructive or overwhelming. By establishing well-defined boundaries and effectively managing our emotions, we can steer these interactions in a direction that not only aligns with our well-being but also fosters understanding and mutual respect. With the right approach, even the most difficult discussions can become opportunities for growth and connection.

Prioritizing Self-Care in the Face of Difficult Interactions

Engaging in conversations with difficult individuals can be both emotionally taxing and a test of our patience. These interactions can often lead to feelings of exhaustion, anxiety, self-doubt, and insecurity. This is where the significance of self-care steps in.

After a taxing conversation, it's imperative to prioritize self-care and give ourselves the space to recuperate. Taking a moment to unwind can come in various ways specific to the individual: maybe it's a quiet moment in bed with a cup of tea, a refreshing walk outdoors in nature, indulging in some self-pampering activities like a manicure or face mask, going to the gym for 30 minutes or even jotting down feelings in a journal. These simple activities can make a huge difference in processing the emotions tied to the conversation and prevent them from lingering or affecting subsequent interactions.

The concept of self-care, and the act of indulging in activities purely for relaxation and enjoyment, should never be underestimated or overlooked. In our fast-paced world, it's easy to dismiss these moments of reprieve as frivolous or non-essential. However, dedicating time to activities that rejuvenate our spirit and calm our mind is paramount. No matter the self-care activity you prefer, these moments of respite are not just luxuries; they are vital for our mental and emotional well-being. By regularly prioritizing self-care, we equip ourselves with the resilience and balance needed to face life's challenges with a clearer mind and a more centred heart.

In the long run, consistently prioritizing our well-being ensures that we remain effective communicators, even when faced with the most challenging conversational partners.

Oops, That Was Awkward: How to Bounce Back from Conversation Fumbles

At some point in our lives, we've all found ourselves caught in the whirlwind of an awkward conversation. Whether it was a surprise run-in with an old friend we've lost touch with, a joke that didn't land as expected, an offhand remark that was taken the wrong way, or simply a moment of silence that stretched a tad too long. These moments can leave us wishing for a quick escape or a rewind button. But what exactly makes a conversation feel awkward?

Awkwardness often arises from unexpected deviations in the flow of a conversation. It's that cringe-worthy moment when our internal alarm bells ring, signalling that something in the conversation didn't go as planned. These moments can be triggered by a myriad of factors. However, it's important to understand that these moments are a universal part of human interaction. Why? Because conversations are dynamic and involve navigating the complexities of human emotions, perspectives, and backgrounds. We're not always going to predict or understand every nuance of the person we're speaking to, and vice versa. Everyone brings their own set of experiences, beliefs, and boundaries to a conversation. Given this diversity, it's only natural that misunderstandings or unexpected turns in a discussion occur. The hallmark of a skilled conversationalist is not avoiding these moments but embracing them as reality and having the resilience and tools to bounce back from these fumbles when they occur.

Ironically, the fear of awkwardness can make it more likely to occur. When we're overly anxious about saying the "right" thing or making a perfect impression, we can become less natural in our interactions, leading to forced or inauthentic exchanges.

However, there is a silver lining. These awkward moments, common as they are, offer opportunities for growth, self-awareness, and even humour. By accepting them as a natural part of communication, we can approach conversations with more ease and confidence, ready to navigate and recover from any hiccups that come our way. After all, it's through these fumbles that we often learn the most about ourselves, others, and the art of conversation.

Graceful Recovery: Turning Awkward Moments into Memorable Ones

Awkward moments in conversations are like unexpected rain showers – they can catch you off guard, but with the right approach, they can be refreshing and leave a lasting impression. Recovering from these moments with grace and humour not only salvages the situation but can also enhance the connection between those involved.

Grace Under Pressure: When faced with an awkward moment, it's essential to remain composed. Instead of panicking or becoming flustered, take a brief pause. This gives you a moment to collect your thoughts and decide on the best course of action.

Maintaining Confidence: Confidence is your anchor in the unpredictable seas of conversation. Even if you stumble, projecting confidence can reassure others and even yourself. If you've said something awkward, instead of retreating into a shell, maintain eye contact, keep your posture open, and continue the conversation. Your ability to remain confident, even when things don't go as planned, sends a message that you're comfortable with who you are, imperfections and all.

Acknowledge the Elephant in the Room: Sometimes, the best way to move past an awkward moment is to acknowledge it. By saying something like, "Well, that was a bit awkward, wasn't it?" or "Oops, didn't see that coming!" you can lighten the mood, share a laugh, and pave the way for the conversation to move forward. This approach shows self-awareness and can make others feel more at ease, knowing that everyone has recognized the hiccup and is ready to move on.

Use Humour: Laughter is a universal icebreaker. Making a light-hearted joke about the situation can quickly turn things around and diffuse the tension. For instance, if you've momentarily forgotten someone's name, you might playfully say, "I promise I remember our entire conversation, just not your name. Mind helping me out?" Using humour not only helps in steering through the awkwardness but also demonstrates your knack for handling situations with grace and wit, making the interaction memorable for the right reasons.

Shift the Focus: If a topic leads to an uncomfortable silence or a miscommunication, tactfully redirect the conversation in a different direction. This doesn't mean disregarding the previous topic, but rather providing a fresh avenue for discussion. Using transitional phrases such as "Speaking of which..." or "On a related note..." can be handy tools. Additionally, bringing up a recent event, asking an open-ended question, or sharing a light anecdote can serve as effective detours, ensuring the conversation continues to flow smoothly.

Apologize if Necessary: Recognizing and owning up to our mistakes is a sign of maturity and self-awareness. If you realize you've said something inappropriate or offensive, it's important to address it promptly. Offering a heartfelt apology not only demonstrates your acknowledgment of the error but also your commitment to maintaining a respectful dialogue. A sincere "I'm sorry" can help rebuild trust and go a long way in mending conversational missteps.

Stay Present: During an awkward moment, it's easy to become consumed by the discomfort and lose track of the ongoing conversation. By staying present in the current moment, actively listening to the other person and engaging, you can shift the energy from the awkwardness back to the heart of the conversation. This not only helps in regaining conversational momentum but also demonstrates your commitment to the interaction. Over time, you'll find that by staying present and engaged, minor hiccups become less disruptive, allowing for more fluid and meaningful exchanges.

Learn and Reflect: After the conversation, take a moment to reflect and analyse the situation. What triggered the awkward moment? Was it a sensitive topic? Perhaps a jest that wasn't well-received? Or maybe a cultural or personal boundary was unknowingly crossed? By pinpointing the cause, you not only gain insight into the dynamics of the interaction but also equip yourself to better navigate similar situations in the future. This self-reflection helps in sharpening your communication skills, ensuring that with each encounter, you become more skilled at manoeuvring the intricate web of human interaction and steering clear of possible missteps with each new encounter.

Remember, everyone has faced and will face awkward moments in conversations. While it's natural to want our interactions to be flawless, it's not the absence of these moments but how we handle them that defines our communicative prowess. Handling them with grace and humour not only showcases resilience but also endears you to others.

Proactive Measures: Strategies to Prevent Conversation Fumbles

Conversations, like any other skill, can be honed and refined with practice and foresight. While it's impossible to eliminate all potential hiccups, there are proactive strategies and measures one can take to reduce their occurrence. Here are some tips to steer your discussions with greater confidence:

1. Prepare and Research: Before heading into a conversation, especially in a professional or unfamiliar setting, do a bit of homework. Understand the context, the people involved, and the topics that might come up. A well-informed conversationalist is less likely to be caught off guard.

2. Active Listening: One of the primary reasons for conversational missteps is not truly listening to the other person. By practising active listening, you ensure that your responses are relevant and considerate of the ongoing dialogue.

3. Avoid Assumptions: Making assumptions can lead to misunderstandings. Instead of presuming you know what someone means or feels, ask clarifying questions. This not only prevents potential blunders but also shows that you care about understanding them correctly.

4. Stay Present: It's easy to get lost in our thoughts or become distracted, especially in today's digital age. By staying present in the moment, you can better gauge the mood, tone, and direction of the conversation, adjusting your responses accordingly.

5. Practice Empathy: By putting yourself in the other person's shoes, you can better anticipate how certain topics or comments might be received. An empathetic approach to conversation helps in navigating sensitive subjects with care.

6. Know Your Triggers: We all have topics or situations that make us uncomfortable or defensive. By recognizing these triggers, you can approach such topics with more caution or steer the conversation in a direction where you feel more at ease.

7. Mind Your Body Language: Non-verbal cues often convey more than spoken words. Being aware of your body language, and reading others', can provide insights into the flow of the conversation and when it might be time to shift the topic or adjust the tone.

8. Practice Makes Perfect: Engage in diverse conversations, challenge yourself to speak in different settings, and practice with people from various backgrounds. The more you converse, the more adept you'll become at moving through human communication.

9. Continuous Learning: Consider reading books, watching videos, attending workshops, or seeking training on effective communication. The more you learn, the better equipped you'll be to handle diverse conversational scenarios.

10. Celebrate Growth: Remember to acknowledge and celebrate your progress. Every conversation, especially the challenging ones, contributes to your growth as a communicator.

In the end, while these strategies can significantly reduce the chances of a conversation fumble, it's essential to remember that everyone makes mistakes. What defines us is not the absence of errors but our ability to learn, adapt, and grow from them.

The Art of the Exit

Every conversation, much like a story, has a beginning, middle, and end. No matter how riveting or insightful the exchange may be, there comes a point where it reaches its natural conclusion. Just as starting a conversation is crucial, recognising when it's time to wrap things up is equally important. This awareness is not just about avoiding overstaying one's welcome, but also about respecting the time and energy of all participants.

Exiting a conversation with grace is a skill that, when mastered, can leave a lasting positive impression. Just as a performer knows when to exit the stage to leave the audience yearning for an encore, a graceful exit from a conversation ensures that the exchange lingers in memory as a pleasant experience. Adding to that, a graceful exit can serve as a protective measure for the relationship. By ensuring conversations don't drag on past their natural endpoint, we prevent potential discomfort, boredom, or misunderstandings. This foresight helps in nurturing and preserving relationships, making future interactions more anticipated and welcomed. In essence, understanding the lifecycle of a conversation and acting upon it is a testament to one's emotional intelligence and social sensitivity.

Recognizing when a conversation is over might seem straightforward, but depending on the context, it can be more nuanced than it appears. Here are some pointers to help you determine when it's appropriate to gracefully wrap things up:

Prolonged Pauses: While moments of silence are natural, extended lulls might indicate that the conversation has naturally wound down. If both parties are struggling to find new topics or are merely rehashing old points, it might be time to move on.

Body Language Cues: Non-verbal signals can be quite telling. If the other person starts looking around the room, checking their watch or phone, or their body is angled away from you, these might be signs that they've tapped out from the conversation and are ready to move on.

Waning Energy Levels: Conversations have a certain energy. When enthusiasm and engagement start to wane, and responses become monosyllabic or repetitive, like "Yeah," "Uh-huh," or "Right," it often means the person is no longer deeply engaged in the conversation and the conversation might have run its course.

External Interruptions: Sometimes, external factors, like an announcement, a phone call, or another person interrupting, can provide a natural pause or end to the dialogue.

Achieving the Conversation's Objective: If the conversation had a specific purpose, like asking a question or seeking advice, and that objective has been met, it's an appropriate moment to end. Likewise, if a topic has been thoroughly explored and there's nothing new to add, it's a clear sign that it might be time to close.

Respecting Time Constraints: If you or the other party mentioned a time constraint at the beginning ("I have to be somewhere in 10 minutes"), be mindful of that limit.

Intuition: Sometimes, it's just a gut feeling. Trust your instincts. If it feels like the conversation has reached its natural end, it probably has.

By being in tune with the ebb and flow of a conversation, one can navigate its course with finesse, ensuring that both parties feel valued and heard.

Sealing the Deal: The Importance of Closure in Conversations

Closure in a conversation serves multiple purposes. Firstly, it signals to the other person that you value the time and topics discussed, wrapping up the exchange in a respectful manner. A simple acknowledgement, like "It was great talking about this with you," or " Thank you for sharing your perspective," can leave a lasting positive impact. A sudden or unexpected exit might leave the other person feeling perplexed or unappreciated, potentially straining the relationship. Secondly, providing closure helps in summarizing and reaffirming the main points or decisions made during the conversation. This is especially crucial in professional settings where clarity is paramount. A brief recap or a simple acknowledgement can go a long way in ensuring that everyone is on the same page. Furthermore, closure sets the stage for future interactions. By ending on a positive note, or even suggesting subjects for future discussions, you create a welcoming atmosphere for subsequent conversations. This is particularly beneficial in networking scenarios where building long-term relationships is the goal. Lastly, for those who might experience social anxiety, having a go-to strategy for ending conversations can be a relief. Knowing how to gracefully end a discussion can boost self-confidence and reduce the stress of unexpected or prolonged interactions.

While it might seem like a minor detail, providing closure is a signature trait of effective communication. It's a nod of respect to the other party, a tool for clarity, and a bridge to future interactions. So, the next time you find yourself in a conversation, remember that how you exit is just as important as how you enter.

Graceful Exits: Leaving Conversations with Tact and Elegance

1. The Time Check: If you're at an event or gathering, you can glance at your watch or phone and mention another commitment. "I'd love to continue this, but I have another meeting to attend."

2. Introduce a Third Party: If you're in a group setting, consider introducing the person you're speaking with to someone else. This can provide them with a new conversation partner and allow you to step away.

3. The Honest Approach: Sometimes, it's okay to be straightforward. If you're feeling tired or overwhelmed or simply don't want to be there, it's perfectly acceptable to say, "I feel a bit drained and need to take a break. Let's catch up later." Additionally, avoid over-explaining. While it's polite to give a reason for leaving, avoid lengthy explanations. A simple reason, delivered with sincerity, is usually sufficient.

4. Offer a Follow-Up: If you genuinely enjoyed the conversation but need to leave, suggest a follow-up. "This has been great. Can we continue this over coffee next week?"

5. Use Body Language: Sometimes, non-verbal cues can signal that you're preparing to leave. Gradually turning your body away from the person speaking, taking a step back creating a significant distance, or gathering your belongings can indicate your intent to exit.

6. Close with Positivity: Regardless of the reason for your exit, always end with a positive statement or express gratitude for the conversation. A simple "I've enjoyed our chat; it was nice catching up" or "Thanks for sharing that with me" can set a positive tone for your departure. This ensures the conversation concludes on a high note.

7. Practice the Exit: Like any other skill, gracefully exiting a conversation can be improved with practice. Try different approaches in various settings and take note of what feels most natural and effective.

Remember, the goal is to exit the conversation in a way that respects both your needs and those of the person you're speaking with. With practice and mindfulness, you can master the art of the graceful exit, enhancing the quality of your interactions and the impressions you leave behind.

The Follow-Up: Keeping the Conversation Going After Goodbye

Conversations, especially meaningful ones, don't always end with a simple goodbye. In fact, the moments after a conversation can be just as crucial as the dialogue itself. The period following a conversation is a pivotal juncture, offering an opportunity to solidify the connection you've established. The art of the follow-up isn't merely a post-conversation formality; it's an intentional gesture aimed at nurturing and deepening the relationship you've begun. By revisiting previously discussed topics, expressing further interest, or simply checking in, you not only demonstrate genuine care but also pave the way for a more profound and enduring connection. This continuity in communication ensures that the seeds of connection planted during the conversation continue to grow.

The Power of a Thank You: After having a meaningful or productive conversation, consider sending a message or email to the other individual expressing appreciation for the dialogue. Whether it was an informal catch-up with a friend or a formal business discussion, a brief "Thank you for taking the time to talk with me" or "I valued our conversation" can go a long way. It recognizes the importance of the exchange and the other person's contribution.

Timeliness Matters: If you've promised to send information, especially in a professional situation, do it promptly. This not only shows reliability but also that you were engaged during the conversation.

Personalize Your Follow-Up: Avoid generic messages. Referencing specific points from your conversation can make your follow-up feel personal and show that you were truly listening. Additionally, use different mediums. While emails are standard, don't shy away from sending a handwritten note, making a phone call, or even sending a relevant article or book recommendation. The medium you choose can add a layer of thoughtfulness to your follow-up, particularly if a specific communication preference was mentioned during your discussion.

Propose a Next Step: If you feel the conversation was particularly engaging and there's more to explore, suggest a next step. It could be another meeting, a coffee catch-up, or attending an event together. No matter what you suggest, stay genuine. Only commit to a follow-up if you genuinely want to. It's essential to remain authentic and not give the impression of being interested if you're not.

Feedback is Golden: Following a business meeting or a collaborative session, offering feedback can be an excellent way to follow up. It shows you've reflected on the conversation and are eager to move things forward.

Regular Check-ins: If you're looking to build a long-term relationship, whether professional or personal, regular check-ins can be beneficial. It doesn't always have to be about something specific. Sometimes, a simple "How have you been?" or "I hope you're doing well," can reignite a conversation.

Respect Boundaries: While following up is essential, it's equally crucial to respect the other person's boundaries. If they're not responsive or show disinterest, it's a sign to pull back.

In essence, a follow-up is an extension of the conversation you've had. It's about showing respect, interest, and the desire to continue building on the foundation you've set. By mastering the follow-up, you ensure that your conversations, no matter how brief, have the potential to blossom into lasting connections.

PART 3

Saying Sorry in Small Talk and Beyond

Misunderstandings, slip-ups, misinterpretations and missteps are all bound to happen when operating in the complex landscape of interpersonal communication. Whether it's a minor oversight in casual conversation or a significant error in judgment, the ability to extend and receive an apology is an essential communication skill. Yet, it's important to note that not every apology carries the same weight or sincerity.

A genuine apology goes beyond the mere utterance of the words "I'm sorry." It encompasses acknowledgement, responsibility, and a commitment to rectification. Firstly, recognizing and admitting the mistake is key. This means being specific about what went wrong. This acknowledgement shows awareness and introspection. It's not just about recognizing that feelings were hurt, but understanding *how* and *why* the actions or words were inappropriate or hurtful. The next step is to assume responsibility. This involves not only recognizing the error but also expressing genuine remorse for the hurt or inconvenience caused. This shows the other person that you're not just apologizing out of obligation but truly feel regretful for your actions. A sincere apology avoids deflecting blame or making excuses. It's about owning up to one's actions without trying to minimize their impact or shift the blame elsewhere. Lastly, a genuine apology often includes a commitment to ensure the mistake doesn't recur. This might mean promising to act differently in the future, making amends, or taking steps to prevent similar oversights.

So, why is perfecting the craft of apology so essential in communication? For starters, it helps repair trust. When someone acknowledges their mistake and takes steps to rectify it, it demonstrates integrity and builds credibility, A well-timed and heartfelt apology can smooth over awkward moments and diffuse tension. This reinforces mutual respect and prevents minor misunderstandings from escalating into more significant conflicts. It shows empathy, maturity, and a willingness to maintain a positive relationship, even when things don't go as planned.

In essence, a genuine apology is a powerful tool that, when used appropriately, can mend bridges, strengthen bonds, and foster a culture of understanding and mutual respect in both casual and professional interactions.

When to Say "Sorry" and When to Hold Back

When it comes to apologies, discernment is key. While saying "sorry" can heal rifts and rebuild trust, it's equally important to recognize when an apology is truly necessary and when it might be excessive or even counterproductive.

Firstly, let's delve into situations where an apology is necessary:

Clear Mistakes or Oversights: If you've made an error, forgotten an important date, or unintentionally hurt someone's feelings, it's time to apologize. Recognizing and admitting your mistake can go a long way in repairing the relationship.

Misunderstandings: Even with the best intentions, miscommunications can occur. If something you said or did was misconstrued, apologizing for the confusion and clarifying your intent can help clear the air.

Intentional Wrongs: If you've knowingly done something hurtful or harmful, it's crucial to apologize sincerely and take steps to make amends.

Now, there are also scenarios where an apology might not be the best course of action:

Over-Apologizing: Constantly saying "sorry" for every little thing, even when it's not your fault, can diminish the weight of your words. It can also portray a lack of confidence or an unnecessary burden of guilt.

To Placate: If you're apologizing just to keep the peace or avoid confrontation, without genuinely recognizing any wrongdoing, the insincerity can often be palpable. Such apologies can feel hollow and may not resolve the underlying issue.

When You Don't Believe It: If you're being pressured to apologize but don't genuinely feel you've done anything wrong, it's essential to evaluate the situation critically. An insincere apology can sometimes do more harm than good.

Apologizing for Being Yourself: If you're expressing genuine emotion, belief, or an opinion respectfully and someone takes offence, you shouldn't feel obligated to apologize for your feelings or beliefs. It's essential to be true to yourself while also being considerate of others.

The art of the apology is a delicate balance. It's about recognizing genuine moments of error and taking responsibility, while also ensuring that you're not using "sorry" as a crutch or diluting its meaning through overuse. Being discerning about when to apologize and when to stand your ground is a crucial aspect of effective and authentic communication.

Tailoring Apologies to the Context

Apologies, while universally recognized as gestures of remorse and reconciliation, need to be tailored to the context in which they are given. The way you apologize to a manager for a missed deadline might differ from how you express regret to a friend for forgetting their birthday. Let's explore how to craft apologies suitable for various contexts:

Professional Settings:

- Tone and Formality: In a professional environment, it's important to maintain a formal and respectful tone. Avoid overly emotional language and focus on the facts and potential solutions.

- Take Responsibility: Avoid passing the blame or making excuses. Instead, acknowledge the oversight and its impact on the project or team.

- Offer Solutions: After acknowledging the mistake, propose a way to rectify it. This proactive approach shows commitment and responsibility.

- Follow-Up: After the initial apology, ensure you follow through with any promised actions to rebuild trust.

Here's an example of an apology suitable for a professional setting:

"Dear Team,

I want to address the error in the recent project report I submitted. I realize now that my oversight led to inaccuracies that may have affected our team's decision-making process. I apologize for any confusion and inconvenience this has caused.

To rectify this, I have already corrected the report and attached the updated version. Additionally, I will implement a more thorough review process for future submissions to prevent similar issues.

I appreciate your understanding and am committed to ensuring the accuracy and reliability of our work going forward.

Sincerely, [Your Name]"

Personal Relationships:

- Genuine Emotion: Personal relationships thrive on genuine emotions. Ensure your apology is heartfelt and sincere.

- Listen Actively: Sometimes, the aggrieved party needs to express their feelings. Listen actively without interrupting or becoming defensive.

- Make Amends: Depending on the situation, consider ways to make amends, whether it's planning a belated celebration or spending quality time together.

- Commit to Change: If a particular behaviour is repeatedly causing hurt, commit to making a change and seek feedback on your progress.

Here's an example of an apology suitable for a personal relationship:

"Hi [Name],

I've been thinking a lot about our conversation the other day and I realize that I hurt you with my words/actions. I am truly sorry for causing you pain – that was never my intention. I understand now how my actions were hurtful and I regret that deeply.

I've been listening to what you said and I want to make things right. Maybe we could [plan a belated celebration/spend some quality time together/do something you enjoy] to start mending things. I also want you to know that I am committed to changing my behaviour. It's important to me that you feel valued and respected in our relationship, and I welcome any feedback you have as I work on this.

I value you and our relationship a lot, and I hope we can move forward from this, stronger and more understanding of each other.

With love, [Your Name]"

Small Talk Situations:

- Keep it Light: In casual settings, the apology doesn't need to be heavy or overly formal. A simple "Oops, my bad!" can suffice for minor slip-ups.

- Quick Recovery: If you've made an awkward comment or a conversational faux pas, acknowledge it with humour and steer the conversation in a new direction.

- Read the Room: If you sense that your comment may have been taken the wrong way, even in a casual setting, a simple "I didn't mean it like that, sorry!" can clear the air.

Here's an example of an apology suitable for a small talk situation:

Imagine you're at a casual gathering and you accidentally spill a drink on someone's jacket. You might say "Oops, my bad! I'm really sorry about that. Let me grab some napkins and help clean that up. [After cleaning] To make it up to you, can I get you another drink? And maybe steer clear of my clumsy self for the rest of the evening? [with a light, humorous tone]"

Or, if you make an awkward comment during a conversation, you might quickly recover with "Ah, that didn't come out right, did it? Sorry about that, I meant to say [corrected statement]. Let's switch gears – have you seen [another topic] recently?"

These examples keep the tone light and offer a quick recovery, helping to maintain the relaxed atmosphere of the setting.

In all contexts, the key to a successful apology lies in its sincerity, the acknowledgment of the mistake, and the genuine intent to make things right. By tailoring your apology to the situation, you ensure that your message of remorse is both appropriate and effective.

The Path Forward: Accepting Apologies with Grace

Accepting an apology is equally as important as offering one. How we respond can set the tone for future interactions and either mend or further strain the relationship. Here's how to graciously accept an apology and pave the way for positive future interactions:

Pay Full Attention: When someone extends an apology, it's essential to be present and attentive. This shows respect and recognizes their attempt to reconcile. Refrain from cutting them off or jumping to conclusions; instead, allow them the space to convey their emotions and explanations.

Recognize Their Effort: A simple acknowledgement like "Thanks for saying that" or "Your apology means a lot" can go a long way. It shows that you recognize their effort to make things right.

Express Your Side: If it feels right, share how their actions impacted you. This isn't to point fingers but about creating understanding. For instance, "I felt very hurt when that happened, but I'm glad we're addressing it now."

Establish Clear Guidelines: If the issue that led to the apology is recurring, it's beneficial to outline your expectations and boundaries for the future, clarifying what is and isn't acceptable. This can prevent future misunderstandings and lay the groundwork for healthier interactions ahead.

Consider the Context: The depth of the hurt and the nature of the relationship will influence how you move forward. For instance, overlooking a detail at work might be easier to move past than a deep personal betrayal. In some cases, accepting an apology might not mean resuming the relationship as it was, but rather finding a new way to relate or deciding to part ways amicably.

Avoid Holding Grudges: Holding onto past mistakes can hinder the growth of a relationship. After an apology has been offered and you've acknowledged it, commit to moving forward. Try and avoid bringing up the same issue in future disagreements.

Rebuild Trust Gradually: Trust, once broken, takes time to rebuild. Be patient with yourself and the other person. Celebrate small milestones and positive interactions as you both work towards restoring the relationship.

Remember, while an apology can mend fences, true healing comes from the actions that follow. Both parties should be committed to understanding, growth, and fostering a positive environment post-apology. By accepting apologies with grace and understanding, we not only strengthen our relationships but also foster a culture of empathy and compassion.

Mastering the Apology: Exercises to Cultivate Sincerity

Apologizing is an art, and like any skill, it can be honed with practice and intention. The goal isn't to become perfect but to cultivate a genuine commitment to healing and strengthening relationships. Below are some exercises and approaches to guide readers in delivering sincere apologies:

1. Self-reflection Exercise: Dedicate some time aside to think about a situation where you might have upset someone. Write down what happened, how you think the other person felt, and your own emotions. Then think about how the situation could have been handled differently or what you would change if you could

go back. Based on your reflections, draft a sincere apology. This activity nurtures empathy and insight, both essential components of a genuine apology.

2. Role-playing: With a trusted friend or family member, practice apologizing for a hypothetical situation. Ask for feedback on your tone, body language, and choice of words. This can help you become more aware of how you come across and adjust accordingly. Additionally, practice rephrasing apologies that use the word "but." For instance, instead of saying, "I'm sorry I was late, but traffic was terrible," try, "I'm sorry I was late. I know it's important to be on time, and I'll try to leave earlier in the future."

3. Active Listening Drill: When someone shares a grievance with you, practice active listening. This means not interrupting, not getting defensive, and truly trying to understand their perspective. This drill can help you become more receptive when someone is hurt by your actions.

4. Feedback Loop: After apologizing, ask the other person how they felt about your apology. This can be eye-opening and provide valuable insights into areas you can improve or are unaware of.

5. Empathy Building: Watch movies or read literature that explores complex human emotions and dynamics. Afterwards, reflect on the narrative, the character's actions, mistakes, and their path to reconciliation. Engaging with such stories can provide a window into the human experience and deepen your capacity for understanding and compassion.

6. Restitution: Think of ways you can make amends beyond just words. Maybe it's helping someone with a task, replacing an item you broke or damaged, or simply spending quality time with them. Practising restitution can reinforce the sincerity of your apology.

7. Mindfulness Meditation: Engage in mindfulness practices. By being present and enhancing self-awareness, you can more readily identify your missteps and address them with genuine contrition and clarity.

8. Seek External Resources: Read books, attend workshops or explore educational resources on effective communication and conflict resolution. Gaining knowledge from seasoned experts can provide valuable tools and techniques for crafting sincere apologies.

Judge Not: The Essential Virtue of Non-Judgment in Conversation

At the heart of human interaction lies a deep desire for understanding and connection. This desire propels us to share experiences, empathize, and forge relationships that enrich our lives. However, amidst these interactions, a significant barrier often emerges and impedes this connection: our inclination to pass judgments. Whether subtle or overt, these judgments can cast a shadow over conversations and create distance even in the most intimate of relationships. But what exactly constitutes a judgmental attitude, and how does it shape the dynamics of our conversations and the quality of our relationships?

Being judgmental involves forming opinions or conclusions about someone based on limited information, often influenced by personal biases, stereotypes, or past experiences. It's a quick assessment, usually made without a full understanding of the situation or the individual. While it's natural for humans to categorize and evaluate as a way to make sense of the world, an excessive or unwarranted judgmental attitude can have profound implications on our interactions and relationships.

Understanding judgmental behaviour means recognizing that it goes beyond merely forming opinions. It's about assigning value—often negative—to someone based on certain behaviours, choices, or characteristics. This can stem from various sources, including societal norms and personal upbringings. For instance, if someone grew up in a household where academic achievements were highly valued, they might judge others based on their educational background. Similarly, if someone was brought up in a family where athletic prowess was highly esteemed, they might be inclined to assess others based on their physical fitness or sports achievements.

When we approach conversations with a judgmental mindset, we're less open to understanding the other person's perspective. Instead of listening to understand, we listen to evaluate, often missing the essence of what's being shared. This can lead to miscommunication or unnecessary conflicts, as we might be more focused on validating our preconceived notions rather than genuinely listening to what the other person has to say. Furthermore, if individuals feel they're constantly being judged, they're less likely to open up or share their true feelings or experiences, fearing criticism or misunderstanding. This can stifle the depth and authenticity of a relationship, making interactions superficial. In professional settings, being judgmental can hinder collaboration and innovation. When team members feel their ideas are prematurely judged, they might withhold valuable input, fearing ridicule or dismissal. This not only limits the diversity of ideas but can also impact team cohesion and productivity. In relationships, constant judgment can erode the foundation of trust. If someone feels they're always under scrutiny, they'll likely become defensive or distant. For deeper connections to form, there needs to be a safe space where both parties can be vulnerable. A judgmental attitude can prevent this level of intimacy from developing. Additionally, being on the receiving end of judgment can reinforce negative self-beliefs, especially if the individual already struggles with self-worth.

To cultivate genuine connections, it's essential to recognize and curb judgmental tendencies. The good news is that being judgmental is a habit that can be changed. By doing so, we create a more open and empathetic approach to conversations. Embracing this type of approach not only enriches our conversations but also strengthens the bonds we share with others.

The Barriers Created by Judgment in Communication

Promotes Defensive Behaviour: Judgment can put individuals on the defensive. Instead of focusing on the content of the conversation, they might become preoccupied with defending their actions, beliefs, or feelings. This defensiveness can lead to arguments, misunderstandings, and further communication breakdowns.

Cloud Objectivity: A judgmental mindset can cloud our ability to see situations objectively. When we're quick to judge, we often overlook crucial details, misinterpret intentions, and jump to conclusions. This lack of objectivity can lead to misconceptions and prevent us from understanding the full picture.

Erodes Trust: Trust is a foundational element of any meaningful conversation. However, consistent judgment can erode this trust over time. If individuals feel they're constantly under scrutiny, they'll be less inclined to share, confide, or seek advice, weakening the bond of the relationship.

Reinforces Stereotypes and Biases: Judgment often stems from deeply ingrained stereotypes and biases. When we allow these biases to dictate our conversations, we miss out on the opportunity to learn, grow, and challenge our preconceived notions. This not only limits our perspective but also perpetuates stereotypes, further hindering open dialogue.

Stifles Growth and Learning: Open, honest conversations are avenues for growth and learning. However, a judgmental environment can stifle these opportunities. Instead of exploring new ideas, challenging our beliefs, or gaining new insights, we become stuck in a loop of validation and criticism.

Creates Emotional Distance: Over time, judgment can create emotional distance between individuals. Feeling judged can lead to feelings of resentment, hurt, or isolation. This emotional distance can make it challenging to reconnect, share, and engage in meaningful conversations in the future.

The Mirror of Judgment: Reflecting Our Inner Struggles

The act of routinely judging others is often less about the person in question and more about our own internal battles. At its core, this behaviour can be seen as a defence mechanism, a way to deflect attention from our insecurities, fears, and perceived inadequacies. By shining a spotlight on someone else's perceived shortcomings, we momentarily divert the gaze from our vulnerabilities, giving ourselves a brief respite from self-scrutiny. However, this diversionary tactic comes at a cost. While it might offer temporary relief from our own self-doubt, it also creates barriers to genuine human connection. When we're quick to judge, we're less likely to empathize, understand, or truly listen to another person's perspective. This can lead to superficial relationships, devoid of the depth and understanding that most of us crave.

Furthermore, this pattern of judgment can stifle our personal growth. Every moment spent critiquing others is a moment lost for self-reflection and self-improvement. Instead of acknowledging and addressing our own areas of growth, we become entrenched in a cycle of external blame and criticism. Over time, this can result in diminished self-awareness, leaving us less equipped to navigate life's challenges and less in tune with our own needs and desires.

While judging others might seem like an external act, it's deeply intertwined with our internal world. Breaking this cycle requires introspection, self-awareness, and a commitment to personal growth. Only by turning the lens inward and addressing our insecurities can we hope to foster deeper, more meaningful connections with those around us.

The Role of Empathy: Suspending Judgment and Understanding Perspectives

Empathy, often defined as the ability to resonate with and understand the emotions of another, stands as a foundational element in the fabric of human communication. It serves as a bridge, connecting different individual experiences, allowing one to momentarily set aside their lens of perception and view the world through another's eyes. This unique quality becomes particularly evident in the context of conversation.

In dialogues, empathy isn't just a passive act of listening. It's a conscious effort to delve into the emotional and cognitive landscape of the speaker, paving the way for a more profound understanding. It's about feeling with the person, not just feeling for them. Connecting with the emotions, motivations and aspirations that drive them. Have you ever confided in a friend or family member, and rather than them simply offering words or advice, they truly shared the emotional journey with you? Such moments highlight that genuine conversations are not just exchanges of words but a deeper communion of souls.

At an individual level, empathy encourages us to re-evaluate our own biases and preconceived notions. By genuinely trying to understand the perspectives of others, we often find that many of our biases are unfounded, leading to more open and impartial exchanges. This approach expands our worldview, challenges our beliefs, and deepens our appreciation of the diverse human experience.

Most importantly, empathy acts as a counterforce to judgment. When we approach interactions with empathy, we prioritize understanding over evaluation. This fosters an environment free from judgment where individuals feel acknowledged and listened to. Moreover, empathy can also act as a healing balm, soothing potential tensions and misunderstandings.

In essence, empathy is a powerful tool in communication. It transforms conversations from mere exchanges of information to deeply resonant experiences. It encourages us to suspend judgment, prioritize understanding, and embrace the diverse mosaic of human perspectives. By practising and applying empathy, we not only enhance our conversations but also champion a world where understanding and unity take precedence over judgment and division.

Practical Strategies for Practicing Non-Judgment in Daily Life and Conversations

Embracing a non-judgmental attitude is a conscious choice that can be cultivated with practice and intention. Incorporating strategies can gradually shift your mindset towards one of non-judgment. Over time, this approach not only enhances your conversations but also enriches your relationships and personal well-being. Here are some practical strategies to help integrate non-judgment into your daily interactions and life.

1. Mindful Awareness: Begin by cultivating mindfulness. This involves being present and observing your thoughts and reactions without acting on them immediately. By recognizing when you're forming a judgment, you can choose to let it go rather than allowing it to influence your behaviour.

2. Active Listening: Focus on truly listening to what the other person is saying without immediately formulating a response or opinion. This allows you to understand their perspective more deeply and reduces the likelihood of jumping to conclusions.

3. Empathy Practice: Try to put yourself in the other person's shoes. By understanding their feelings, backgrounds, and perspectives,

you can approach conversations with more compassion and less judgment.

4. Challenge Your Initial Thoughts: Before forming an opinion, take a moment to assess if you have all the information. Many times, judgments arise from partial information or misconceptions. By seeking clarity, you can avoid unnecessary judgments.

5. Examine Your Biases: When you sense a judgment forming, delve into its origin. Reflect on why you hold that particular view about someone. Consider its source: is it a valid observation or perhaps a projection of your own feelings or experiences?

6. Limit Negative Influences: Surround yourself with positive, open-minded individuals. If you constantly engage with negative or judgmental people, their attitudes can rub off on you. Seek out environments and communities that promote understanding, unity and acceptance.

7. Reflect on Past Judgments: Think about times when you've been judgmental in the past. What triggered it? How did it affect the conversation? Reflecting on these instances can provide insights into your triggers and help you avoid them in the future.

8. Affirmations: Use positive affirmations to reinforce your commitment to non-judgment. Phrases like "I choose to understand rather than judge" or "I embrace all perspectives with an open heart" can serve as daily reminders.

9. Educate Yourself: Engage with diverse cultures, beliefs, and lifestyles. The more you learn about the world and its myriad of perspectives, the less likely you are to judge what you don't understand.

10. Practice Forgiveness: Remember that everyone, including yourself, is human and prone to mistakes. Instead of holding onto

grudges or judgments, practice forgiveness. This applies to self-forgiveness as well; recognize when you've been judgmental, learn from it, and move forward.

The Most Interesting Person in the Room: How to Become Fascinating to Others

We've all witnessed it: at a gathering or event where amidst the hum of conversations, there's that one person who naturally draws others in. Their stories enchant, their insights provoke thought, and their laughter is contagious. They're not necessarily the loudest or the most extroverted, but there's an undeniable magnetism about them. But, how? What's their secret?

This chapter explores the artistry of genuinely captivating others, emphasising that the goal isn't to seek attention for self-centred reasons but to become the best versions of ourselves and elevate our social interactions to its highest potential. The good news is that being interesting isn't reserved for a select few. Through mindfulness, consistent effort, and a genuine desire to connect, anyone can elevate their interactions, making every conversation an opportunity to inspire and be inspired.

The Power of Passion

In this human game, certain individuals stand out and leave a lasting impression. More often than not, it's not just their accomplishments or physical appearance that draws us in (though those can be factors), but something deeper: their passion. Being deeply invested in a passion or cause can ignite a spark within you, making you a magnet for others' attention.

Passion, in its truest form, is an intense zeal or fascination for a specific topic or mission. It's an energy, a dynamic force that motivates individuals to learn, grow or explore. When someone speaks with passion you feel it. Their eyes light up, their gestures become more animated, and their voice carries a certain conviction. This genuine enthusiasm is infectious, drawing listeners in and making them want to learn more.

One of the perks of having a deep-seated passion is the wealth of knowledge it brings. When you care about something, you naturally invest time in understanding it. This degree of knowledge allows for richer, more nuanced conversations. You can bring depth and lucidity to conversations, introducing others to novel ideas or viewpoints. It goes beyond merely presenting facts; it's about intertwining narratives, personal experiences, and unique insights that provide a refreshing outlook. Additionally, those driven by passion often engage in activities aligned with their interests, be it community involvement, attending workshops, travelling, or just about anything else. These experiences provide a reservoir of anecdotes and lessons that can be shared in conversations.

But it's not just about being a good talker. Passion also makes one a keen listener. When you're genuinely interested in a subject, you're more likely to seek out others who share that interest, leading to mutual exchanges of knowledge and experiences. This reciprocity in conversation fosters a sense of connection and understanding. Furthermore, having a cause or passion signifies a sense of purpose. It shows that you stand for something and that you're driven by values and principles. This can be especially captivating in an age where many are searching for meaning and purpose in their own lives.

With all this said, it's important to approach conversations with humility. While it's great to share your passion, it's equally important to be open to others' perspectives and interests. After all, the goal is mutual connection and understanding, not a monologue.

In conclusion, while many factors contribute to making someone "interesting," passion holds a unique power. It's a bridge that connects the heart and mind, making conversations resonate on both an intellectual and emotional level. So, whether it's cars, environmental conservation, paper clips, or any other subject, digging into your passions not only fulfils your life but also makes you a captivating presence in any room.

A Life Worth Talking About

One of the most captivating things about a person is not just what they say, but the experiences that fuel their stories. At the heart of every fascinating conversation is a life lived with zest, curiosity, and action. Sharing stories of our adventures, the lessons from our missteps, and the joy of our discoveries make us relatable, memorable, and, yes, fascinating.

Acting on things we love or enjoy isn't just about personal fulfilment, though that's a significant benefit. It's also about accumulating a wealth of experiences that can be shared with others. It's about diving deep, getting our hands dirty, and truly living life. Whether it's travelling the world, joining a combat sports class, moving to another city, or simply quitting the job you hate, these experiences add layers to our persona.

Moreover, real-life experiences bring authenticity to the table. These stories, when shared, resonate deeply because they come from a place of truth and personal growth. The emotions are more genuine, the details more vivid, and the narrative more engaging. There's no need to embellish or exaggerate; the truth speaks for itself.

So, if you find yourself yearning to be the most interesting person in the room, start by living a life that's worth talking about. Dive into your passions, seek out new experiences, and do the things you've always wanted to do. Take the step and embrace the unknown. In doing so, not only do we become more interesting conversationalists, but we also lead a life that's fulfilling and rich in memories, all the while inspiring others to embark on their own adventures. After all, the best stories come from a life well-lived, and there's no better time to start crafting those tales than now.

The Lifelong Learner

Never stop learning. The most captivating conversationalists are often those who embrace a mindset of continuous education. They understand that they are a student of life and learning is never complete. This allows them access to an array of topics to delve into during discussions at any moment. Staying up to date on a variety of subjects, from the latest technological advancements to cultural phenomena, historical events, or even popular entertainment, broadens the number of people you have access to and can connect with.

Moreover, being well-informed signals to others that you're curious, open-minded, and invested in understanding the world around you. It showcases your adaptability and your willingness to engage with new ideas. It's not just about accumulating facts though. Continuously learning fosters critical thinking and the ability to view topics from multiple perspectives. This depth adds layers to your conversations and allows for discussions that go beyond surface-level chatter.

In essence, dedicating yourself to continuous learning doesn't just amplify your knowledge base; it also elevates your conversations, making them resonate more deeply. Whether it's signing up for an online class or just keeping abreast of the latest news, each piece of knowledge you acquire enhances your conversational arsenal.

Conclusion

The Journey of Connection

As we come to the end of this exploration, it's essential to remember that the journey to becoming a captivating conversationalist is just that—a journey. It's not about reaching a destination or achieving a state of perfection, but about continuous growth, understanding, and connection.

Throughout "*Small Talk, BIG Impact*" we've delved deep into the intricacies of human interaction. We've unearthed the power of genuine listening, the magic of storytelling, and the undeniable pull of charisma. We've tackled the barriers that often stand in our way, from anxiety to self-doubt, and we've equipped ourselves with tools to navigate the vast seas of social interaction. But beyond the techniques and strategies, the heart of meaningful conversation lies in genuine human connection. It's about seeing and being seen, understanding and being understood. It's about recognizing the shared humanity in each of us, and the profound ways in which our stories intertwine.

As you venture forth, equipped with the knowledge and insights from this book, remember that every conversation is an opportunity. Embrace each interaction with an open heart and a curious mind. Celebrate the successes, learn from the missteps, and always strive to deepen your connections. And whenever you find yourself in a conversational quandary, don't hesitate to revisit these pages for guidance and inspiration.

So, take a deep breath, muster your newfound confidence, and be proud of who you are. Dive into the beautiful dance of small talk and remember that in every brief exchange lies the potential for something enduring and unforgettable.

Thank you for embarking on this journey with me. Here's to a world filled with richer, more meaningful conversations and connections that last a lifetime.

THANKS FOR READING!

I have thoroughly enjoyed writing this book, and truly hope you've enjoyed it and found value in it. If you have, it would be greatly appreciated if you could head over to Amazon to leave a review!

This really helps small publishers like myself be seen. Reader feedback lets me know how I've done and what I can improve on to serve you in my next book!

Simply scan this QR code with your phone or device, and you will be taken to the book's review page.

Alternatively, to leave a review:

- Head over to the book's page on Amazon or find it through your recent purchases
- Scroll down towards the bottom of the page and click on the button that says "Write a Customer Review"
- You can simply leave a star rating out of 5 or write a short review!

Thanks! Your support is greatly appreciated!

Made in the USA
Coppell, TX
22 July 2024